Pirates, Buccaneers, and Gentlemen Adventurers

Pirates, Buccaneers, and Gentlemen Adventurers

E. O. Hoppé

SOUTH BRUNSWICK AND NEW YORK:
A. S. BARNES AND COMPANY
LONDON: THOMAS YOSELOFF LTD

© 1972 by A. S. Barnes and Co., Inc.
Library of Congress Catalogue Card Number: 70-126944

A. S. Barnes and Co., Inc.
Cranbury, New Jersey 08512

Thomas Yoseloff Ltd
108 New Bond Street
London W1Y OQX, England

ISBN 0-498-07783-7
Printed in the United States of America

Contents

	Introduction	7
1	Henry Morgan and the Plunder of Panama	13
2	The Buccaneers: Freebooters of the Spanish Main	22
3	In Defense of Captain Kidd	26
4	The Narrow Borderline: Privateer or Pirate?	35
5	How Did Men Become Pirates?	37
6	Blackbeard: The Terror of the Seas	44
7	The City of Sin	59
8	"Gentlemen" Pirates	62
9	Where to Seek Hidden Treasure	67
10	Deadlier than the Male: A Trio of Bloodthirsty Wenches	72
11	"Long Ben": The Colorful Account of Captain John Avery	86
12	The "Jolly Roger" Flies from the Main Mast	91
13	A Quartet of Sea Hawks	103
14	Gallant John Lafitte	111
15	Frederick Misson: The Good Pirate	114
16	Pirates in All but Name	121
17	Postscript	131
	Types of Old Seagoing Craft	132
	Bibliography	133
	Index	135

Introduction

Piracy dates back to a remote period of recorded history. References to it are found in Homer's epic poems which were probably written more than two thousand years before the birth of Christ.

Down to the time of the Roman Empire the depredations caused by bands of pirates from the north coast of Africa had caused enormous havoc to the coastal trade and their habit to hold captured sea passengers to ransom had become a serious menace. From the classics comes the story of Julius Caesar's seizure by them, his release and subsequent pursuit and capture of them.

Piracy continued to threaten society from the eighth century onwards and well past the middle ages. The Vikings in the north of Europe harassed and plundered the ships of England and France and devastated towns and settlements, and in the south the Barbary pirates had become the scourge of the Mediterranean.

In England the Elizabethan adventurers, men like Hawkins, Raleigh, Drake and others, sailed forth in their small vessels of a few hundred tons' burden to explore unknown oceans and, incidentally, waylay the huge unwieldy treasure-laden galleons of the Spaniards. When such attacks were committed in times while an uneasy state of peace existed between England and Spain, they clearly amounted to acts of piracy, but while the government formally frowned on the deeds, it secretly condoned them.

During the first few decades of the seventeenth century, the Buccaneers moved into the picture. Originally hunters of wild cattle on the islands of Tortuga and Hispaniola, they had turned themselves into a well organized fraternity of sea-robbers. Filled with an intense hatred of Spain which had persecuted them for a century, they attacked and looted treasure ships and ransacked cities all along the Spanish Main.

In the Western hemisphere piracy flourished to an unprecedented extent. It had spread to the Caribbean where the indented coastlines of the numerous islands which form the West Indian Archipelago afforded ideal shelter for the marauders' light sailing craft. From these they swooped down upon passing trading vessels and retreated with ease to their hideouts, as the cumbersome merchantmen could not pursue them through the tortuous and shallow channels that led to their haunts.

It is hard to say what drove men to piracy. There may have been many reasons. In the main its ranks were recruited from all sorts of desperate outlaws and felons fleeing from justice and swarming to the New World, attracted by the opportunities which the West offered to acquire riches quickly. Sometimes circumstances of their past lives may have forced men of hitherto blameless character to take the fatal step; sometimes it was a love for sheer excitement and a carefree life.

After each war the navies disbanded their fighting crews and many sailors, finding themselves unemployed, were compelled to sign on with any captain who offered a berth without looking too closely into his reputation among seafaring folk.

Another cause of the captain of a privateering vessel

turning to piracy was his failure of having met with any ships which he was entitled to attack and plunder under the authority of the "letter of marque" issued to him by his government.

Unscrupulous though the pirates were, a certain lurid glamor clings to them that compels reluctant admiration. Authenticated records tell tales of their splendid daring and of deeds of valor often in face of seemingly overwhelming odds.

But rumor and fiction have often clouded facts and stripped of all romantic aroma the cold truth—that the vast majority of these picturesque villains were utterly ruthless, unprincipled and notorious for the atrocities which they committed. They all preyed upon ships of every kind, irrespective of their nationality, and squandered their ill-gotten spoils in riotous living.

It was not until the first quarter of the nineteenth century that robbery on the high seas was finally brought to an end by the combined determined action of the British and American navies.

We owe much of our knowledge of these strange and desperate men to John Esquemeling, the Dutchman, who served as ship's surgeon with some of the noted pirates and took an active part in their exploits. He tells tales of villainy and treachery, of heroism and of selflessness towards their comrades, of unbounded courage and of bravery. Another chronicler of the days of piracy in the Caribbean and along the American Atlantic Coast was Captain Charles Johnson, who has recorded lurid details of the exploits of many of the most infamous sea-robbers of his time around the turn of the seventeenth into the eighteenth century. Nothing is known of his origin and it is assumed that Johnson must have been a member of the fraternity himself, judging by the intimate knowledge he displays in writing of the deeds of some of the most notorious rascals. It is more than likely that he adopted the name of Charles Johnson as a nom-de-plume, to cover his real identity.

Pirates,
Buccaneers, and
Gentlemen Adventurers

1
Henry Morgan and the Plunder of Panama

As fine a gang of murderers and cutthroats as ever sailed the Caribbean; that was John Esquemeling's opinion of his fellow pirates when Morgan's fleet sailed from Tortuga on an easterly wind.

Not that he was any better himself. He was only just beginning to regret that love of adventure and desire for easy money which had caused him to become a pirate. He moved to where Henry Morgan stood beside the helmsman.

It was the year 1671. For months Morgan, feared throughout the New World as a barbarous and ruthless monster capable of the most fiendish atrocities, had been assembling the largest fleet which those waters had seen; his purpose being to attack the city of Panama.

At that time Panama was a fabulous place to which came the golden galleons from the mines of Chile and Peru, their treasures being transported across the Isthmus and loaded onto Spanish armadas at San Lorenzo on the east coast.

"A good wind and a fine fleet, captain," said Esquemeling.

"Aye," Morgan leaned over the side and spat into the rushing water.

He was a large bulky figure; his chin clean-shaven but his hair hanging in long curling locks and his upper lip adorned with a moustache. His eyes were as wide and blue as a girl's—and could be as cold and piercing as an Arctic wind.

"Thirty-seven ships and two thousand men," he said. "We'll make fine pickings in Panama. You'll not be sorry I made you my chief surgeon—especially when you get your share of the loot," he looked back at the billowing sails of the other ships. "What think you of our little armada?"

Esquemeling eyed him shrewdly and estimated how far he could go in the expression of opinion.

"They're typical of our breed," he answered. "Scum from the gutters of Europe's slums. The world's outcasts."

"And there's you, eh?" Morgan laughed, and slapped him on the back. "Now I must go below and have another look at my maps of the Isthmus."

When he had gone the helmsman grinned at Esquemeling. He knew he could talk to the Dutchman on reasonably familiar terms.

"This Panama, is it really as wonderful as they say?"

"So I believe," Esquemeling replied. "There are reputed to be two thousand fine houses built of cedar, all richly furnished and belonging to wealthy merchants."

"And the church of San Jose, does it have an altar of solid gold?"

"Not solid," Esquemeling corrected, "but covered with plates of beaten gold."

"Good enough. It'll fetch a fancy price." The helmsman licked his lips.

Westward with straining sails the pirate fleet moved

nearer to its goal. Aboard every ship hopes of great wealth were as high as the bright blue sky above them. But many were destined not to return; and those that did were to receive but paltry reward for the hardships ahead of them, followed by treachery and betrayal, while for Morgan the Monster there was to be a knighthood and a colonial governorship!

Ten more days saw the fleet in sight of the castle of San Lorenzo, which guarded the mouth of the Chagres River. As the ships run up the skull and crossbones the Spanish cannon opened fire.

Morgan, realizing that he could not prevent messengers being sent to warn Panama, knew that he must take the castle and press into the interior as quickly as possible.

Accordingly, he sailed into the tiny port with his ships in open formation, all guns firing. It was beyond the capacity of the castle's armament to fire upon more than a few ships at a time.

Soon the leading vessels were under the guns of the fortress and the crews were leaping overboard into shallow water to wade ashore and storm the ramparts. Within an hour the castle had fallen—at a cost to the attackers of 200 killed and 4 ships sunk.

The following day Morgan commandeered a fleet of canoes from nearby Indian villages and set off up the Chagres River with 1400 men, leaving the rest to guard the castle and ships. Against the advice of Esquemeling no food was taken.

"There are plenty of settlements along the river from which we can take food," Morgan said confidently.

But it was not so simple. Not only were the settlements deserted but everything that could be of use to the pirates had been removed—including food.

By the third day they were starving and greeted with shouts of glee the news brought by an advance party that a Spanish ambush lay ahead. At least the soldiers would have food that could be taken.

But again disappointment. The Spanish, outnumbered, fled; leaving in their encampment nothing but some empty leather bags.

Leather, however, was all that these ravening sea-wolves needed. Drawing their knives they slit the bags into strips, soaked them in the river and beat them between stones, then roasted and ate the stuff with frequent gulps of water.

Morgan decided that the time had come to leave the canoes and advance inland.

They soon found and travelled along the much-beaten track by which the gold and silver of South America was carried to the east coast—the Golden Road.

On the fifth day another abandoned settlement was found but this time a small quantity of food had been left. On the sixth day they came upon a barn full of maize which they ate raw. And on the ninth day their empty stomachs were temporarily forgotten when, from the crest of a hill, they saw the vast Pacific.

Morgan pointed to the coast. "We've not far to go. Panama is but a few miles away. And here is food—look!"

Below them lay a lush green valley, fat with grazing cattle.

"Get them," Morgan commanded, "and some of you light fires."

Of the scene that followed Esquemeling wrote in his diary that it was like a cannibal feast, with the pirates gobbling chunks of half-cooked meat and the blood running down their beards.

Later that evening they came in sight of the church spires of Panama.

Shouting gleefully the pirates blew trumpets and beat drums, and were answered by cannon fire from the city walls.

"Back to the trees, lads!" Morgan shouted, "we can wait till dawn."

Out of range they sheltered in the forest and ate the rest of the meat from the valley.

In the light of torches that night Morgan conferred with his captains. His eyes sparkled with the lust for battle. His long hair was matted and greasy but his moustache was still neatly trimmed and his chin shaven.

"According to reports," he said, "these fool Spaniards have put most of their guns at this side of the city. They were warned that we were coming this way so they reason we shall attack from this side. The idiots! In the dawn we march round to the other side where the ground is open but soft for their horses. There, with no cannon behind them, they'll have to come out in the open. They won't have time to transport their cannon from one side of the city to the other."

"How many men do they have?" Esquemeling asked.

Morgan looked at him. "Three thousand," he replied. "They are two squadrons of cavalry and four regiments of infantry."

One of the captains whistled. "I didn't think they had so many."

Morgan gave him a thunderous glare. "We have come too far to have timid feelings," he sneered. "I want two hundred good marksmen. They will advance with muskets, dropping to one knee, firing, then going forward again. The rest of us will fire over their heads as they kneel. Any objections?"

No one had any. Morgan's methods of dealing with men who had objections were too well known; and the captains knew that, so far, the pirates would follow Morgan.

At dawn the Scourge of the Caribbean led his small army to the far side of the city. Here the Governor of Panama emerged at the head of his three thousand men. There were also to be seen a herd of bulls attended by Indians.

"They are supposed to spread havoc among us," commented Morgan grimly. "We'll see about that!"

Shouting "Viva le Rey" (Long live the King!) the cavalry advanced.

Esquemeling later described the battle in his diary. "The field being full of quags and soft underfoot they could not ply to and fro as they desired. The two hundred buccaneer marksmen who went before, every man putting one knee to the ground, gave them a full volley of shots, wherewith the battle was kindled very hot.

"The Spanish foot endeavoured to second the horse but were constrained by the pirates to separate from them. The Spanish then drove the bulls forward but most of them fled in disorder, being scared by the noise. The few that did break through were easily shot. After two hours the Spanish horse was in ruins, almost all being killed. The rest fled with the foot.

"The pirates could not follow immediately, being much harassed and wearied by the long journey they had lately made. Such of the fugitive Spanish as were caught were killed without mercy along with the wounded. Some friars were taken prisoner and brought before Captain Morgan; but he, being deaf to their lamentations, commanded them to be immediately pistoled."

Within a few hours Morgan had learned from a captured officer how the city was defended and soon the pirates were attacking at several points. Fighting was fierce for some time as the Spaniards made their last desperate stand. But by sundown Panama had fallen.

The city was in flames and Morgan afterwards blamed the Spaniards for setting it alight but Esquemeling knew differently. He saw his chief tossing torch after flaming torch into the fine cedarwood houses, his wide eyes glaring madly and voice hoarse with the shouting of orders.

Victory soon brought some disappointments. Although much treasure was found a great deal had been removed or hidden. Even the gold altar in the church of San Jose had apparently been replaced by a plain white one. Not until long afterwards did the priests scrape off the white paint and reveal the gold altar beneath!

Morgan sent search parties in all directions and these returned with prisoners who were fiendishly tortured to make them reveal the hiding places of treasure.

Soon only the yells of drunken, looting pirates and the screams of the tortured rose from Panama's smoking ruins.

Esquemeling improvised a surgery in a church, and for some days was often red with blood to the elbows as he amputated smashed limbs and cut away gangrene.

Discovering that a galleon commanded by one Don Peralta, laden with the ornaments of many churches, had sailed the previous night, Morgan put a crew on board a large ship found caught in the mud and sent it in pursuit; but the pirates spent the night at sea in a drunken orgy and the chance was lost.

"All right," said Morgan, "make me a list of all people whom we hold and who seem to be wealthy. I'll estimate how much ransom we can expect. A lot of them will have friends and relatives in those settlements along the coast. We'll send out a few captives to spread the news of how much we want."

Esquemeling went about his task and gradually ransom began to trickle into ruined Panama. But after a few weeks it was obvious that no more wealth could be wrung from what was left of the city. With a train of 175 treasure-laden mules and 600 weeping and wailing men, women and children who were being held to ransom, they returned to San Lorenzo.

When Morgan divided the loot there were rebellious mutterings that the chief was keeping plenty to himself.

But Morgan, sensing mutiny, had no desire to wait until it happened. In the night a messenger came to Esquemeling where he slept in the castle, the fleet not being ready to sail until the next day.

"Captain Morgan wants you," the messenger said.

Esquemeling found the captain on his flagship in the moonlight, surrounded by a dozen men whom he recognized as being Morgan's oldest and closest comrades.

"We're leaving," Morgan told him bluntly, "and we're taking every ship with us. I've got a few chosen men on all the other ships now. The entire camp's asleep—they're mostly drunk with all the wine we brought from Panama. In the morning they'll be in a mood to slit my throat, and the throats of those known to be nearest to me. So we're going. You can come or stay—please yourself."

Esquemeling knew he had no choice, that if he refused to go he would be killed on the spot.

"Thanks, captain," he grinned. "I knew you wouldn't forget me."

Silently the entire fleet stole across the harbor. They were well out before someone gave the alarm and angry shouts mingling with futile shots faded behind them.

The fleet made for Jamaica where Morgan expected a warm welcome from the Governor, who had secretly financed his expedition; but when he visited the Governor's mansion the pirate chief was furious to find himself arrested and charged with having broken the treaty of friendship which temporarily existed between Britain and Spain.

Sent to England in chains the terror of the Spanish Main was about to go on trial when Lady Luck came to his aid as many times before. War broke out with Spain. Immediately King Charles II gave Morgan a Royal Pardon, a knighthood and sent him back to Jamaica as Lieutenant Governor!

His orders were to hang every pirate he could capture and this Morgan did with relish. Many an old comrade died on a Jamaican gallows, the order of execution signed by His Excellency the Governor.

And Esquemeling? He, sickened by the cruelties that he had witnessed, returned to his native Holland, became deeply religious and wrote his memoirs of the days when he sailed with Morgan to seek the plunder of Panama.

2
The Buccaneers: Freebooters of the Spanish Main

Why buccaneers?

The name comes from the Carib word "boucan" meaning a place for smoking meat, and it was French settlers in the islands who learned the trade from the Indians, who were skilled in the practice of curing the raw flesh of cattle by drying it in the sun, and then smoking it over a smoldering wood fire.

Those Frenchmen were among a colony which lived on the island of St. Christopher together with English settlers when the Spaniards came to drive them out.

Escaping to the coast of Hispaniola (today's island of Haiti and Santo Domingo) they settled for a while.

But peace was not to be their destiny. . . .

The tyrant Spaniards came again and once more the fugitives fled—this time to the island of Tortuga, north of Hispaniola.

The island was called Tortuga because of its shape, which is like that of a tortoise—in Spanish *tortuga de mar*. It was then heavily wooded and abounded in wild cattle.

"We bid you welcome to our island," said the few Spanish settlers who lived there. "May we live in peace together."

And for a while they did live in peace; but as more and more refugees arrived the Spanish became alarmed, fearing that the island would be overrun with foreigners, so some of them sent to the Governor of Hispaniola for help.

Soldiers came and drove the French and English into the forest from where they escaped to the mainland. There they carried out guerrilla war but returned to Tortuga on hearing that English soldiers sent to their aid by the Governor of St. Kitts had landed on the island with guns and ammunition.

More refugees arrived from other European countries, adding to the growing jealousy of Spain. For close on forty years the ownership of Tortuga changed hands many times in a series of takings and retakings.

Once firmly established the buccaneers built forts and strongholds and graduated from "cowkillers," as the Spaniards called them, to sea robbers.

Hatred of Spain combined with a thirst for adventure caused these hunters of cattle to turn seaward.

The island was easy to defend; its many inlets and narrow channels between submerged coral reefs gave secure passage to the light craft of the buccaneers but were too narrow for the cumbersome, slow-moving Spanish galleons.

There was also good shelter from storms and concealed anchorages for the repairing and careening of ships.

Swooping out from the network of branching creeks they preyed upon unsuspecting merchantmen passing along the ocean highway, carrying on the commerce of the West Indies.

As the strength of the buccaneers grew they fitted out

fleets of heavily armed vessels manned by reckless, daring men, causing havoc to shipping and ravaging cities on the mainland. It was the beginning of that organization known and dreaded as "the Brethren of the Main."

All types of men attracted by the freedom of the wild life and the chances of making a fortune flocked to Tortuga. Differences of social status were forgotten.

Laws and articles of association were drawn up. Each member swore to carry out the orders of the council, to obey their leaders, to observe rigid discipline and not to desert. Any violation of the oath met with severe penalties, often either death or expulsion from the Brotherhood.

Booty was divided among crew and officers on an agreed scale. All swore not to conceal anything but to turn every article of loot over to the common fund.

Curious as it may seem, these unprincipled men kept to a strict code of honor in their dealings with each other, and would often divide their share with less fortunate comrades.

The early buccaneers started their career as privateers, preying upon the enemies of their country under government license.

It was a rewarding profession. The thrill of hunting down merchant ships and seizing their cargo was not easily forgotten.

Boldly those sea captains followed the examples of Drake and Hawkins in earlier times, when those Elizabethan heroes had sailed in their caravels of only a few hundred tons burden to face the mysteries of unknown seas in pursuit of the plate-laden galleons of Spain.

What kind of men were those freebooters who enrolled under a chosen leader on the chance of making a fortune?

Seafaring men nearly all; hardy mariners who had served on merchantmen and deserted because of the poor pay; adventurers attracted by the freedom of a daring life; deserters from the Navy; men of a dozen tongues and races—French, Dutch, English and others.

There were slaves who had run away from their masters; strange characters into whose past it was nobody's business to enquire. One common bond united them all—hatred of Spain, which had been mistress of the Caribbean for too long.

Many of the seamen were remarkably fine navigators; men of reckless courage and daring in face of overwhelming odds, bold, not over scrupulous, at times savage, sometimes chivalrous in treatment of prisoners.

The buccaneers reached the height of their power during the period 1671 to 1685. Their successes culminated in Morgan's advance on Panama and the plunder of the richest town in the New World.

But the structure which held the confederacy together had begun to totter and the different nationalities became increasingly divided.

The Brethren broke up after their last great exploit—the sacking of Cartagena.

3
In Defense of Captain Kidd

Mutiny!—on board the ship of Captain Kidd, one of the most notorious of seventeenth-century privateers.

Ruthless and villainous—or so he was reputed—Kidd stood on the deck of the *Adventure Galley* and faced an angry rabble led by gunner Moore who thirsted for the captain's blood.

The ship drifted slowly in calm waters north of Madagascar, and a few miles off its port beam lay the Portuguese vessel which Kidd had just refused to attack.

"It is a peaceful craft," he'd told his crew, restless from a year's voyaging in which they had captured only two prizes.

"What are you afraid of?" Moore sneered. "We've got a Royal Commission as a privateer, and who's to know what happens out here, anyway. We want money. Two prizes in a year isn't enough. What say you, men?"

A roar of approval backed him up. Kidd looked at him with contempt. "Dirty dog of a mutineer!"

Moore reddened with rage, whipped out his cutlass and rushed at the captain. Swift as lightning Kidd seized a nearby tar bucket and smashed it against Moore's head. The mutineer sprawled backwards onto the deck, his cutlass rattling away into the scuppers. He was dead!

It was the end of the attempted mutiny. Deprived of their leader the crew backed down; but even so the situation was too perilous for Kidd to ignore completely their resentment, and shortly afterwards he consented to attack and loot a richly laden Moorish vessel. At his trial he maintained that his life was threatened by his crew.

Captain William Kidd is pictured in history as a sinister figure; around him have been woven countless tales of buried treasure and unspeakable crimes. Popular fiction has painted him as a ruthless scoundrel who deserves no sympathy. But the evidence indicates that Kidd was a brave and resourceful privateer guilty of no proven crimes. Instead he was used as a tool by rich and unscrupulous people and framed at a trial in which the evidence was rigged against him.

"This man is a simple and artless person of unblemished character and has enjoyed a great reputation for honesty," said a witness for the defense.

Such commendations could not save this doomed figure. Behind his judges were powerful forces that had decided on his death.

William Kidd was a native of Dundee, the son of a Puritan minister. He was known as an honorable sailor who had won recognition for seamanship as the commander of privateering vessels during Britain's war with France.

It was in the year 1696 that Kidd was approached by Lord Belmont, Governor of New England, who was on a visit to Britain at the time.

Belmont was an Irishman of tainted reputation. He had been involved in a scandal in London and influential friends arranged for him a governorship in the American colonies to get him out of the way.

"I have formed a syndicate," Belmont told Kidd. "Our purpose is to finance an expedition to chase and capture pirates and such other craft as are the King's enemies, and, of course, to relieve them of their booty. We would like you to captain our ship."

Kidd knew that such a venture could be highly profitable. All along the Atlantic coast, throughout the Caribbean and in the Far East also, the damage done to merchant shipping by pirates was vast, and great wealth could be expected from the capture of such ships.

"Who is in your syndicate?" asked Kidd cautiously.

Belmont smiled. He mentioned Colonel Livingstone, a prominent New York merchant; the Earl of Orford, the Earl of Romney, the Duke of Shrewsbury—and even Lord Somers, First Lord of the Admiralty. With such distinguished names Kidd must have thought that there could be no possibility of treachery. Little did he know of the world of English politics!

"We shall draw up special articles," Belmont said, "stating that all captured goods: jewels, gold and silver ornaments and monies are to be divided at the rate of one tenth to the Government and nine tenths to the syndicate in which you will have three shares."

Kidd agreed, and was given his Royal Commission under the Great Seal of England issued by King William III to his "beloved friend, William Kidd" to apprehend pirates.

A clause in the agreement stated that if no prizes were to be taken neither he nor the crew were to receive any payment. It was this clause which was later to prove fatal to him.

The ship in which he was to sail was the *Adventure Galley*, a sturdy sloop of 287 tons with 34 guns mounted on its upper deck.

Disaster, however, occurred right at the beginning. Many of the 80 men whom Kidd had carefully selected for character and reliability, and some of whom had served under him on previous expeditions, failed to report for duty on the eve of departure.

Coming out of a tavern where they had been roistering they were pounced upon by a Naval press gang and never heard of again.

Was this just an unfortunate coincidence? Possibly, but the presence in the syndicate of the First Lord of the Admiralty raises a suspicion of conspiracy to deprive Kidd of men in whom he could trust. Now he was forced to recruit a motley crowd of men of doubtful character.

The powerful East India Company had agreed to support the venture, but they withdrew on hearing that Kidd's most trusted men had been taken from him. They were wise!

Kidd sailed for Madagascar, hoping to meet pirate or French vessels on his way to that island. Luck, however, was against him. He cruised for almost a year in search of ships which he was commissioned to attack but found none.

Provisions were running low. The crew were disgruntled. The chances of success seemed remote.

Too long now they had endured the sea's song and the wind's lash. Too long they had eaten salted bully beef and known that, according to the terms of the agreement, this was all that they would ever get if no prizes were found. The mood was black.

To prevent open rebellion Kidd gave way to the demands of his crew to hold up a small native vessel at a Red Sea port and forcibly to take some bales of corn and coffee after her captain had refused to sell them. It was his one illegal action and he freely admitted it at his trial.

Sailing south he met at last a ship that hoisted the French flag and seized it as his commission entitled him to do. He sold the cargo and continued toward Madagascar. It was then that he came upon the Portuguese ship and had to quell the mutiny led by Moore.

Then—good luck! Two Moorish vessels were sighted.

"These are ours," Kidd exclaimed. "Look! They have raised the French colors. Give them a shot across the bows."

The vessels surrendered and Kidd boarded them. He found each captain to be in possession of a French pass and carefully put these away. Had he been allowed to produce those vital passes at his trial they would have saved him from a charge of illegal capture.

Kidd decided that one of the captured craft, named the *Quedah*, was a much better ship than the *Adventure Galley*, being of 450 tons and more seaworthy. Accordingly he transferred everything to the *Quedah*, making it his flagship.

Evil fortune now fell upon Kidd. On arrival at Madagascar he found a notorious pirate vessel, the *Resolution*, laying at anchor. It was commanded by Robert Culliford, who had a price on his head.

Kidd ordered his men to board and seize the ship but nearly a hundred of them refused to obey, threatening to kill some forty of the loyal crew. Having locked them below deck they deserted and joined Culliford.

This meeting with the *Resolution* was indeed a lucky one for Culliford, but it proved fatal to Kidd, who was later accused of being friendly with a notorious pirate.

Having taken on more crew Kidd was about to return to Boston when news reached him from the American colonies. He had been declared a pirate! Furthermore, all sea robbers who surrendered before a certain date were offered a free pardon.

Not suspecting Belmont of treachery Kidd decided to sail for home. Had he really been guilty of piracy he would never have done so.

On the return journey he captured a French vessel near Hispaniola and took a valuable cargo. Arriving at Long Island he heard with dismay that the free pardon did not apply to him. He sent for James Emmet, a maritime lawyer, and asked his advice.

"Let me report your arrival to Lord Belmont," advised the lawyer. "His lordship will surely protect you from these charges."

Kidd took this advice—and placed himself in the hands of those who had already decided to destroy him to save themselves.

Rumors had spread about people in high places being involved in unsavory privateering ventures, and a Government committee had been set up to inquire into the facts. Those involved were preparing to sacrifice Kidd and were closing their ranks for this purpose.

The main charge to be made against Kidd was that he had seized illegally the two Moorish ships, and it was vital to get from him the French passes.

Emmet was sent back to Kidd with a request that he let Lord Belmont inspect the passes. Kidd delivered them up in good faith; and his doom was sealed the moment he parted with them. Belmont sent the passes immediately to the Admiralty.

What happened to those passes? No one knows; but

the next time they were seen was two hundred years later when they were found in an old volume of the House of Commons Journals. Had they been produced at the trial they would have cleared Kidd completely—but nobody wanted that.

Belmont sent to Kidd a letter, part of which read as follows:

> Mr. Emmet delivered me two French passes taken on board the two ships which your men rifled, which passes I have in my custody and I am apt to believe they will be a good Article to justifie you. Mr. Emmet also told me about the value of 10,000 pounds in the Sloop with you, and that you have left a ship somewhere off the coast of Hispaniola in which there was to the value of 30,000 pounds more which you had left in safe hands.
>
> I have advised with His Majesty's Council and showed them this letter this afternoon, and they are of opinion that if your case be so clear as you (or Mr. Emmet for you) have said, that you may safely come hither. I make no manner of doubt but to obtain the King's pardon for you.
>
> I assure you on my word and on my honour I will performe nicely what I have promised.
>
> YOUR HUMBLE SERVANT

When Kidd went to see Belmont a few days later he found constables awaiting him.

"You are under arrest!" said the officer-in-charge.

Kidd drew his sword and tried to escape by rushing into the house but they pursued him and he was arrested in Belmont's presence. Shortly afterwards he was sent under strong guard to London.

In May, 1701, the long-drawn-out trial began at the Old Bailey. Much of the evidence was circumstantial and consisted of reports of atrocities committed by sea robbers, none of which had anything to do with his case.

The chief figure behind the farcical proceedings at

the trial was Belmont himself as organizer of the expedition. But neither he nor any other member of the syndicate were called to give evidence.

What was the reason for all this? It can only have been because there were rumors of shady dealings by members of the Whig Government; and the trial of Kidd provided a useful means whereby the opposition party could charge his employers with corruption.

Kidd was tried first for the alleged murder of gunner Moore and it did not take long to convict him of this crime. A formidable group of lawyers was arrayed against him but he was even refused his own counsel!

Early in the trial Kidd was asked did he wish to question a witness.

"It signifies nothing to ask questions," he replied. "Rogues will swear anything. I desire counsel to speak for me."

Mr. Coniers, Crown Counsel, replied: "We admit of no counsel for him."

Kidd turned to the six judges. "I beg that I may have counsel admitted and that my trial be put off. I am not yet ready for it."

"Nor never will be if you can help it," was the sour reply of Sir Salathiel Lovel, Recorder of London and a man notoriously incompetent.

A Colonel Heweson, who had known Kidd for many years, pleaded earnestly for him.

"I have known this man as a person of straight and honest dealings," he said. "The captain consulted me himself before accepting Lord Belmont's offer because he was reluctant to do so."

"Why was he reluctant?" Coniers asked.

"He had received veiled threats by the noble lord that

his own brigantine might be refused clearance papers on her next sailing. It is my belief that he was intimidated."

For expressing this opinion the Colonel was censured by the Court.

The proceedings throughout the trial were a mockery of justice. Kidd was condemned solely on the damning evidence of witnesses chosen by the prosecution and brought to testify against him on promise that their own lives would be spared.

Among these were men who, on their own admission, had deserted him at Madagascar and joined the pirate Culliford. Crew members who remained loyal were declared unreliable and refused a hearing.

Kidd's pleadings for Lord Belmont to give evidence were ignored as were his repeated requests for the two vital French passes to be produced.

When sentence was passed and he was asked if he had anything to say Kidd replied in a few words.

"I have been sworn against by wicked and perjured people."

On the morning of 23rd May, 1701, Captain William Kidd went to the gallows. A good man foully done to death by rogues in high places.

The foremost of those rogues, Lord Belmont, afterwards said: "I deplore my lack of judgement in having trusted an unscrupulous man who deceived me with wicked treachery!"

Perhaps Lord Belmont's greatest crime is that he gave to Captain Kidd a reputation for villainy which has persisted for nearly three hundred years. It is time the record was put right.

4
The Narrow Borderline: Privateer or Pirate?

What was a privateer?

During the seventeenth and eighteenth centuries the practice of carrying on private wars was known as privateering.

The men engaged in this activity were licensed by their governments to prey upon the shipping of enemy nations. These semi-legal ventures were effective weapons in wars which were waged without scruples on both sides.

The type of craft used in these ventures were, as a rule, merchant vessels that had been converted into armed sloops, often under the command of gentlemen-adventurers who had seen service in the Navy and, disbanded after a war, found themselves out of work.

While huge fortunes could be, and were, often made, the hazards were great, and if a venture was unsuccessful, neither captain nor crew received any payment. However, in spite of the risks involved, there were always sailors eager to sign on as the pay in a merchant vessel was poor and the prospect of lining the pocket with gold was tempting. It was not entirely a short-cut to wealth, either, that caused men of good family and respectability to sell their estates and invest the money in such ventures, but also the glamor that was attached to them.

It happened from time to time that a privateer overstepped the boundaries imposed by the Letter of Marque that he held, and committed an act of near-piracy which profited the Government. Although his deed was not officially recognized he was rarely reprimanded.

In practice the borderline between the legal privateer and the true pirate was narrow. Both had the same intention—the gaining of wealth. One cannot tell where one stopped and where the other began.

To the privateer all ships sailing under the flag of an unfriendly nation were objects for plunder; the pirate had no such reservations—to him any richly laden ship, whatever its nationality, was fair prey. According to Nelson all privateers were "no better than pirates," although this sweeping statement must be taken with a grain of salt.

A Letter of Marque was a document signed by the King or head of state giving the holder authority to hunt down and plunder at any time ships belonging to nations with whom they were at war.

These government licenses to prey upon and capture enemy property were granted freely to profit-seekers, mainly to wealthy merchants or noblemen of means who were prepared to fit out and arm vessels at their expense for a purpose which was no less than legalized sea-robbery. In those times the concept of what was right and what was wrong differed from ours.

The practice of granting Letters of Marque extended well into the nineteenth century and was only abandoned by agreement among all the European powers, except Spain, in the year 1856.

5
How Did Men Become Pirates?

At the conclusion of each peace treaty between warring European nations there were always large numbers of sailors and fighting men without work. Circumstances forced them to join the crew of any captain who called for recruits, without asking whether he was an honest seaman.

A captain known to be a successful raider had only to spread the news that he was fitting out an expedition to attract less honest sailors to join him.

There were also lone, resolute men who started out on their careers as sea-robbers in a very humble way. Sometimes it was no more than a stolen shallop in which they would, singlehanded, paddle along a coastline and, joined by a companion or two, board a vessel, killing the watch.

Cruising thus, the budding pirates would gradually get together the nucleus of a fleet which enabled them to prey on bigger fry.

It is hard to say what caused men of all ages and different nationalities to turn to piracy as a livelihood. Some were of high birth and good education; others, the majority perhaps, came from the working-class.

Deserters from the services; English youths shipped to the colonies and later released from bondage to planters to whom they had been sold in payment for their passage from Europe; fugitives running from justice; disgruntled sailors who had jumped ship in some harbor, dissatisfied with the low wages paid in a merchant vessel—these were some of the many who were prepared to join the ranks of the pirates. The temptations were considerable.

Some men turned to the free and easy life for sheer love of adventure and excitement, some were influenced by circumstances of their past lives, while still others engaged in it because of a spirit of rebellion against strangling conventions.

Were these men criminals or gallant adventurers?

It is impossible to say—one cannot explain these things.

The terms pirate and buccaneer are often regarded as meaning the same thing. Although both were sea-robbers their conduct differed in one vital respect and it is necessary to draw a distinction between them.

The pirates were gangs of lawless ruffians who roved the oceans preying upon all shipping irrespective of their nationality, as long as the cargo made it worth while. The buccaneers, on the other hand, confined their activities in the main to the Caribbean where they attacked only Spanish vessels or ransacked only Spanish towns.

As far as one can gather from recorded facts there does not seem to be any evidence to back up hair-raising tales of wholesale tortures and brutalities committed by pirates as a fraternity.

Many of these uncouth ruffians, the majority even, were notorious for their utter want of humanity and would inflict barbarous cruelties to extract confessions or information from prisoners or hostages. They could show a fiendish ingenuity in devising methods of torture: to cut the victims' lips or ears off or slit up their noses; to put burning matches between the fingers; to hoist them up with thumbs and big toes bound together with thin cords and a fire lit below the bodies. Those who died quickly were lucky. The pirates thought nothing of setting prisoners adrift in a small boat or dumping them ashore on an uninhabited island.

Many of these ghastly stories are probably true although they may have been embroidered with bloodcurdling details in the telling. Yet, in a curious way, the majority of these sea-robbers, who feared neither God nor men and recognized no law but their own, were brave and daring and showed a stoical disregard for their own lives.

Forced to live a life of constant alertness, they often endured incredible hardships and faced death unafraid. They rarely gave themselves up and died fighting to the last. More often than not some of these sea-dogs, when captured and condemned to the gallows, bragged about their deeds with the hangman's rope around their necks.

There is some fascination in the boldness with which such daredevil spirits have performed brilliant coups in face of great odds which have never been equalled.

They compel reluctant admiration for their sheer boldness. Their swift and agile sloops could get the better of the clumsy purple-sailed galleons and lumbering merchantmen, run in close and maneuver themselves into a favorable position to engage the enemy at close quarters, broadside to broadside.

Often a pirate captain, when hailed and challenged to show his colors, would hoist the flag of a neutral nation to deceive the oncoming stranger before running up the dreaded black bunting, if it was his intention to assault, seize and plunder the vessel.

Before an attack, the captain addressed the crew and gave to each member his special job. Fighting was furious and reckless, heedless of loss by blazing musket or blasting cannon fire. Men went down giving and expecting no quarter. When hard pressed or even near to destruction they battled on until the enemy hauled down his color or until superior forces overwhelmed them.

After a successful battle the captured vessel was usually scuttled or burned and, if prisoners were taken, they were transferred to the pirate ship bound in ropes and flung into the hold. If the damage done to the hull, sails and rigging was not serious they were repaired, the vessel was manned by some of the pirate crew and added to the captain's fleet.

Pirate crews never received wages but each member was allotted a fixed share in the plunder of any captured ship in accordance with a fixed scale. There was also compensation for any member injured.

All members of the crew, including the officers, were bound by a solemn oath not to hide or keep anything for themselves, to turn all loot into a common fund and to obey their leaders.

It was the remarkable honor and loyalty among themselves that kept these vicious men together in a bond of unity—aware, no doubt, that their very existence depended upon faithfulness with one another and that only thus could they survive.

There were always some black sheep who were not above turning against their comrades to save their own skins, but they were the exceptions and it was not often that promises were broken. There were no distinctions of social status.

The Caribbean waters, from the Bahamas to the Guinea Gulf, swarmed with pirate craft, spreading terror among legitimate traders. No merchant vessel could be sure to pass unmolested. A very effective system of intelligence informed the raiders of dates when and where ships carrying rich cargoes would sail.

Along the great sea-lanes their sloops and schooners would lie in wait to swoop down upon merchantmen homeward bound for England or Spain, laden with spoil. Their merchandise consisted of spices from the East, bales of silk and wools, jewels, pearls and precious metals, golden doubloons, hogsheads of rum and kegs of brandy worth many thousands of pieces of eight.

Craft of all sorts were fair game—stately, unwieldy galleons and swift agile clippers, great square-rigged vessels and lumbering merchantmen, poops and schooners, three-masted barques, and on occasion open shallops or low, flat galleys,* when bad luck deprived them of the capture of more valuable prizes.

The island-studded coasts of the Caribbean with their maze of sea and land-locked bays and calm lagoons were ideal hiding places in which pirate fleets could beach, careen their ships in between marauding expeditions, refit and take in supplies, food and water.

In such places they sought refuge when pursued by heavy men-of-war and from here they emerged on receiving news of the sailing of rich galleons and heavily laden trading craft.

The island of Jamaica in the West Indies was in name

---
*See: Description of Sailing Craft.

a respectable British colony but was, in fact, completely dominated by the pirate fraternity. The harbor town of Port Royal was the headquarters of some of the most notorious sea-robbers in history, as described in another chapter. It was the principal market where merchants came to buy goods without asking awkward questions as to their origin.

In spite of treaties signed by Britain and Spain guaranteeing to respect each other's territories in the New World and vigorously to suppress all assaults against ships and settlements, the buccaneers continued their semi-legal attacks on Spanish property.

To Spain's complaints that it had broken the treaty, Britain's usual reply was that "His Majesty's Government never gave any letters patent, nor commissions for acting any hostility against the subjects of the King of Spain."

In 1716 Britain took determined steps to stamp out pirating in the Caribbean by sending a formidable fleet of Navy vessels to the West Indies. However, the results were ineffective and it was expected that a Proclamation of Pardon, issued by King George I in the following year, would be more successful. This Proclamation granted a free pardon to all pirates who surrendered themselves by a fixed date. A good many marauders accepted the King's act of grace but quite a number eventually returned to piracy.

Many of the pirates died a violent death after a lifetime of seafaring. The number of those who grew rich upon their spoil and spent a respectable old age was small.

Near Wapping, on the river Thames, close to the steps known as "Execution Dock" stood a post from which the bodies of executed pirates were suspended in chains, exposed to the incoming tides.

Even in these days acts of piracy are recorded.

Not many years ago an American citizen was found guilty of piracy and sent to jail for three years.

In Indonesian waters a tribe of fierce Muslims, the Saluks, carry on the tradition of sea-robbers, harassing and looting junks which ply between Borneo and Celebes. No less than 80 different attacks in the course of one year (1961) have been recorded by the authorities.

In 1951 a Chinese motor vessel shelled and boarded an English freighter off the Shanghai coast, holding the 19 European passengers as hostages. A few years later the British steamer *Wing Song* was fired on by an armed motor junk off the China coast. Three Europeans were held in their cabins and released after a payment of ten thousand dollars. It has been reported that the pirates treated their prisoners with extreme courtesy.

6
Blackbeard: The Terror of the Seas

In the darkness, the solitary light on the pirate ship swayed gently. Every eye aboard the man o' war watched it. Yet there was no sound, across the water, of men forced in desperation to turn and fight off an enemy.

The man o' war tacked slowly about.

"Down anchor!" came the whispered command. "No need to let the pirate know the King's ship is so near."

The naval officer rubbed his hands in pleasure.

"This time, eh, this time! We'll have him now!" he murmured.

So great was the excitement on board that no one slept for fear the pirate's light dancing out there might be gone by morning.

But when the first cold light of dawn came trailing up over the horizon, a shout of anger brought the captain from his cabin.

The "ship" that had held them there all night was nothing but a long pole stuck in an old ship's barrel, with a lantern fastened to the top of it. Once more Blackbeard had outwitted his pursuers!

Edward Teach, known as Blackbeard, the "Terror of the Seas," was a native of Bristol. For three years he had terrorized the West Indies, plundering and burning any luckless ship that crossed his path.

It was in 1716 that he first came to the notice of the

King's ships. Serving under another infamous pirate, Captain Benjamin Horngold, young Teach was placed in command of a captured sloop.

Bitter fighting followed in which the young sailor showed such boldness and daring that Horngold offered him a share in his next adventure, and together they set out in the spring of 1717 for Carolina.

Plundering a brigantine and several smaller ships they also captured a merchantman while passing the bar off Charleston, and found a rich cargo of wine, gold bullion, provisions and silks.

So profitable was the cruise that the pirates sailed for the West Indies, where the sea and landlocked bays and inlets afforded perfect hideouts.

Lying in wait until they sighted a heavily laden ship they set all their canvas before the wind, chased her and ran the dreaded Black Flag to their mast.

A broadside crashed into the victim's main topsail, bringing it in flames down onto the deck. A short running fight followed but the pirates were soon masters of the broken ship which turned out to be a French Guineaman with a rich cargo.

At this time a Free Pardon was offered to all pirates who gave up their crimes by a certain date. King George issued this proclamation in an attempt to free the seas of the rogues who preyed on honest ships.

"I have finished," said Horngold, showing Teach a copy of the Proclamation. "His Majesty promises that we can keep the treasures we have taken so I shall accept the Free Pardon."

Thus he parted company from Teach and sailed his ship to New Providence where he and his crew surrendered to the Governor.

Teach, now known as Blackbeard, took possession of the French Guinea-man, mounted her with forty guns taken from various prizes, and renamed her the *Queen Anne's Revenge* and manned her with the toughest hands from Horngold's crew.

Setting course south-east towards the Windward Islands he met a large ship, the *Great Allen,* near St. Vincent. The pirates plundered her, marooned the crew, then set fire to the ship and left her burning to the waterline.

Fresh victims followed. Looming out of the dawn mist a trim vessel suddenly bore down upon the pirate. She was the *Scarborough,* a British man o' war of thirty guns, out on a routine pirate-hunting expedition.

Blackbeard licked his lips like a tiger seeing a hearty meal, and with colossal impudence, ordered "Hoist the Jolly Roger! Prepare to fire!"

Hour after hour the battle raged, with the man o' war steadily gaining on the pirate. Then, a lucky shot from one of the pirate's cannon hit the Englishman near the waterline, ripping a large hole through the planking.

With water pouring into the crippled vessel the captain of the *Scarborough* was forced to realize that his pumps could hardly cope. He was forced to stand away and limp back to Barbados, leaving a triumphant Blackbeard.

Recklessly he now set sail for the South American coast, and by the time of his arrival in the Bay of Honduras, the news of the pirate's victory over the man o' war had gone ahead. "The Terror of the Seas" they named him.

Nearing Turneffe the *Queen Anne's Revenge* fell in with a sloop captained by Stede Bonnet, a gentleman of previously respectable character, formerly a Major in His Majesty's forces, now pirate by choice.

It was a meeting of souls. Blackbeard and Bonnet joined forces.

Blackbeard soon discovered that his new partner had little knowledge of navigation.

"I am always getting lost," Bonnet laughed, as they drank one evening in Blackbeard's cabin.

The pirate chief raised his bushy eyebrows.

"So! That is bad. How say you that we put my own chief mate, Richards, in command of your ship, and you live at ease here on mine?"

Bonnet, easy-going and already dominated by the far stronger personality, agreed without argument.

While both ships lay at anchor off Turneffe, taking on fresh water, the lookout man sighted a sloop making for shore. Richards sailed out in Bonnet's ship to intercept her.

When he hoisted the Black Flag the captain of the other ship immediately surrendered, not daring to take on a pirate in battle. She was the *Adventure,* lately out from Jamaica.

Blackbeard took her captain and crew aboard his own ship, putting some of his men, under Israel Hands, on the captive sloop.

Emboldened by success, and now having a fleet of three ships, Blackbeard sailed for the Bay of Honduras, hoping for further victims. He was not disappointed.

Near Trujillo he encountered a merchantman, the *Protestant Caesar,* accompanied by four sloops. When Blackbeard broke the Black Flag at his masthead and fired a warning shot across the bows of the merchantman, all hands abandoned ship and rowed ashore in one of her boats!

Blackbeard transferred the booty to his own ship, put

a party aboard the *Protestant Caesar* and a sloop, and set fire to the others.

He then spent some time in Havana. By now his reputation had spread far, and by all accounts he was a formidable creature: a huge powerful man of immense strength with abnormally long, ape-like arms.

He was credited with being able to strike a man down with his cutlass and fling him overboard with one hand. His savage looks were increased by jet-black, shaggy hair which covered his bull-like face.

It was his custom to twist the ends of his thick beard, which fell to his waist, into small pigtails and tie them together over his ears, giving him a weird and devilish appearance.

When going into action he used a trick which terrified his opponents. Untying the ends of his beard from behind his ears, he plaited his whiskers also, and stuck twisted hempcords dipped in saltpetre into them, as well as under his hat. Then, during the fighting, he would set them alight so that they dangled about his face like fiery snakes.

To complete the full war paint he wore a scarlet sash wrapped around his waist and slung over one shoulder in which he carried an arsenal of weapons, consisting of daggers and cutlasses and three braces of pistols hanging in holsters.

Charging into battle in full cry, brandishing pistols or flourishing knives, long arms whirling, he was a fearsome sight, striking terror into all who dared oppose him.

From Havana Blackbeard returned to his lair in the Bahamas, where he repaired and refitted his ships. Then, having received word that a large ship bound for London was about to leave Charleston, he sailed for the Carolinas, and lay off the bar for six days.

Capturing the Englishman was easy. As she carried a number of prominent Charleston citizens among her passengers, Blackbeard decided to use them as hostages.

The following day he coolly took a brigantine and a sloop in full view of the town. There were eight other ships in harbor ready to sail, but not one of them dared to leave for fear of being seized by the pirates.

"Look at them!" Blackbeard exulted. "Terrified of me—and well they might be!"

Daringly he sent a party ashore with the medicine chest under the leadership of Richards. His surgeons had reported a shortage of medicines.

The shore party took with them a Mr. Marks, one of the hostages.

"You are to tell Governor Johnson," Blackbeard had ordered, "that if the chest is filled and my men return safely I will then release the hostages."

The Governor stormed when Blackbeard's outrageous demand was brought to him, but his hands were tied. Many of his friends and fellow members of the Council had relatives on board the pirate ship. Reluctantly he had to fill the pirates' chest with drugs and ointments.

For once Blackbeard kept his word. The captives were sent ashore, but only after being robbed of all their jewelry and gold and silver.

From Charleston Blackbeard sailed to North Carolina with his fleet, which now consisted of his flagship the *Queen Anne's Revenge,* Major Bonnet's *Revenge,* a sloop and a smaller vessel which served as a tender.

Greed had now taken possession of him. Although he had already amassed a fortune he had no intention of sharing his booty.

Pretending that the ships needed overhauling, he ordered them into a sandy creek, where he deliberately ran his own vessel aground.

Israel Hands, in command now of Major Bonnet's ship, was in Blackbeard's confidence, and he proceeded to carry out his part of the plan. By pretending to go to the help of the grounded ship, he succeeded in grounding his own.

Blackbeard then went aboard the small tender with a crew of forty, leaving his own ship and the *Revenge* broken on the rocks, with those he wished to be rid of marooned on a small island.

Charles Eden, Governor of North Carolina, was on friendly terms with some pirate captains. In those days it was common for respectable men to grow rich on a "sleeping" partnership in piratical ventures.

Blackbeard, knowing this, decided to make a wily deal with Governor Eden by taking advantage of the King's Proclamation, and pretending to renounce piracy in return for a free pardon.

Calling on the Governor he had a long talk with him and the result was that Blackbeard and twenty of his men received their certificates of a free pardon for their past crimes, declaring them to be "henceforth good and worthy citizens and subjects of His Majesty."

"Are you going to settle down, captain?" Richards asked him.

"Settle down!" Blackbeard sneered. "There's rich picking ahead, my lad. Just you wait."

For some time he stayed ashore, living in quiet luxury, biding his time. So sober and penitent did he appear that a Court of Admiralty, which he persuaded Governor Eden to hold, declared him not to have been a pirate at all, but an honest privateer!

Blackbeard's lavish spending and hospitality, together with his generous gifts of rum and barrels of sugar, attracted many of the leading men of the colony to his fine mansion near the town of Bath, close to Ocracoke Inlet where, on the Governor's permission, his ships remained at anchor.

Thus, all through the ages—including the present day—have evil men spread bribery and corruption among those in high places who were only too eager to be bribed and corrupted.

Blackbeard was a ruffian at heart, and could not resist taking treasures from the houses of friends, and even to insult their womenfolk.

His popularity began to vanish, and hatred took its place, even though he still had the backing of his powerful friends.

Tough scoundrel though he was, Blackbeard was also an excellent actor, and dressed with gay elegance, always wearing the most fashionable clothes from his extensive wardrobe, most of them probably taken from his many victims.

Swaggering in full-skirted, brocaded coats and silk-embroidered waistcoats, wearing costly jewelry (also stolen), a rakish hat cocked on his immaculate periwig, he cut a dashing figure.

It was now, probably to improve his image of respectability, that this villain married sixteen-year-old Prudence Lutrelle, only daughter of a planter's widow.

Urged on by her mother, who was flattered by the attentions paid to her daughter by this wealthy and colorful personality, the girl was swept off her feet by dreams of the grand life that she imagined she would have when married to him. The wedding ceremony was performed by his faithful crony, the Governor.

The young bride's happiness did not last long. After only a few days of marriage Blackbeard took her on board his sloop where he put her in chains and locked her in his cabin, allowing no one to see her.

He then sailed along the coast and, in the darkness, at anchor off Plum Point, ordered six of his men ashore with him. They staggered across the sand carrying a heavy iron chest and picks and shovels.

"Now, dig here!" Blackbeard ordered, at a desolate spot on the beach.

By the light of lanterns a pit was dug and the iron chest lowered into it. After rolling a huge boulder over the freshly turned sand the party returned to the ship.

On deck Blackbeard faced the party sternly, his bearded face threatening in the lantern glow.

"What you have done here tonight you will forget. Understand? Else I'll slit all your throats—slowly!"

The men swore hastily that they would indeed forget, and the ship sailed away.

Why Blackbeard murdered his bride of only a few days no one knows, but it can be guessed that perhaps she overheard some of his plans for the future, and he decided that she knew too much.

Cruising north Blackbeard met three English ships from which he took only provisions. He was after bigger game.

Nearing the Bahamas, he captured two French sloops bound for Martinique, but allowed one to go free. He put the crew of the captured sloop on the free one, but her rich cargo of cocoa and rum and sugar he transferred to his own ship. He then hurried back to North Carolina and went immediately to see Eden.

The result of his visit was that a special court decided that the Martinique ship was a lawfully taken prize, since he swore on oath—backed by Eden—that he had found the ship adrift, abandoned by her crew!

For this help Governor Eden found himself the richer by sixty hogsheads of sugar, and his secretary, Tobias Knight, by twenty barrels!

There was still some danger for the Governor. The Martinique prize lay at anchor in the harbor, but there was a possibility that some other ship might come in and identify her. How to get rid of such unwelcome evidence?

Blackbeard declared that the ship was leaking and might sink, thereby endangering other shipping. He was formally ordered by the magistrates to sail her out to deep water, fire and sink her. Thus he destroyed all evidence of his crime with full permission from the people supposed to stop piracy!

Vengeance, however, was on the way for Blackbeard—and justice, too!

His misdeeds were becoming too obvious. The insolence and scandalous behavior of his ruffians were causing alarm among the planters. Knowing they could expect no help from Governor Eden they sent a secret deputation to Governor Spotswood of Virginia, and asked for his help.

Spotswood, an honorable and law-enforcing man, was so indignant at the tales of undisguised piracy and corruption, that he agreed to send two well-armed sloops commanded by Lieutenant Robert Maynard to hunt the pirates.

In the silent darkness two Virginian flat-bottomed sloops sailed down the James River until they reached the narrow gap in the 100-mile-long sand bar that encloses the Pamlico Sound, known as the Ocracoke Inlet. Inside the bar Blackbeard's ship lay at anchor.

The sloops carried only small arms—poor defense

against the heavy guns of their quarry—but Lieutenant Maynard was a man of great courage, and determined to rid the world of a monster.

In his pocket he carried Governor Spotswood's proclamation:

> By His Majesty's Lieutenant Governor, and Commander-in-Chief, of the Colony and Dominion of Virginia.
> Publishing the Rewards for Apprehending or Killing Pyrates.
>
> Whereas, by an Act of Assembly, made at a session of Assembly, begun at the Capital in Williamsburgh, the eleventh day of November, in the fifth year of His Majesty's reign, entitled an Act to Encourage the Apprehending and Destroying of Pyrates: it is, amongst other things enacted, that all and every person or persons, whom, from and after the fourteenth day of November, in the Year of Our Lord One Thousand Seven Hundred and Nineteen, shall take any pyrate or pyrates ... shall receive ... the several awards following; that is to say, for Edward Teach, commonly known as Captain Teach or Blackbeard, one hundred pounds; for every other commander of a pyrate ship, sloop or vessel, forty pounds; for every lieutenant, master or quartermaster, boatswain or carpenter, twenty pounds; for every other inferior officer, fifteen pounds, and for every private man taken aboard such ship, sloop or vessel, ten pounds; and, that for every pyrate that shall be taken by any ship, sloop or vessel belonging to this colony or North Carolina ... like rewards shall be paid according to the quality and condition of such pyrates ... And, I do order and appoint this Proclamation, to be published by the Sherriffs at their respective County houses, and by all Ministers and Readers in the several Churches and Chapels throughout this colony.
>
> Given at Our Council Chamber at Williamsburg, this 24th day of November, 1718, in the fifth year of His Majesty's reign.
>
>   GOD SAVE THE KING.
>   A. SPOTSWOOD.

Scoundrel and cutthroat though he was, Blackbeard

possessed a fierce animal courage, and showed complete disregard for his own safety. It was this quality that finally brought about his doom.

In the early dawn, Lieutenant Maynard's sloops slipped quietly into the inlet where the pirate ship heaved gently on the water.

Surprise, however, was no longer possible; Blackbeard's lookouts had warned him.

"We will board her straight off," the Lieutenant decided.

It was a brave decision, for the odds were formidable, but his men were well disciplined in hand-to-hand fighting at close quarters, and the Lieutenant knew that this was his only chance for success.

The sloops were now within gunshot range of the pirate ship.

"Hoist the Ensign!"

The shout echoed over the still water.

Almost at the same time as the King's Colours rose to the masthead, the dreaded Skull and Crossbones appeared at the mast of the pirate.

Then, with a thunderous crash and billowing smoke, a cannon roared out at the King's ships.

Blackbeard had stripped his vessel, clearing his decks and running back the great cannon to be loaded. He now slipped anchor and faced directly towards the two sloops. His intention was to run them down with as much speed as his great sails could give him.

The great ship bore down heavily upon the smaller ones, and then—disaster! With a slow grinding noise and a long shudder she went aground on a sand bar!

A piece of luck indeed for Maynard, but victory was still not in sight.

Heavy cannonfire from the temporarily disabled pirate crashed about the two sloops, causing great casualties among the crews.

The sloops returned the mighty bombardment with what feeble fire they could; and by clever maneuvering Lieutenant Maynard managed to draw near the pirate bow before she floated off the bar, thus getting out of range of her vicious cannon.

Slowly his ships sailed nearer, nearer, until with barely a hundred yards to go, the great pirate ship began to swing round with the incoming tide, round until she was broadside again to her attackers.

With a ferocious roaring, cannon blasted across the small space between the ships, riddling one of Maynard's sloops fore and aft, totally disabling her.

Maynard continued to advance in his own sloop, gaining steadily on the enemy. As the two ships came within hailing distance, Blackbeard's voice roared defiantly.

"Damn you, you villains. Who are you? And whence came you?"

"You may see by our colors we are no pirates," was the calm answer.

"Damnation seize my soul if I give you quarter, or take any from you!" bellowed the pirate at the Lieutenant, whose cool reply: "I do not expect quarter from you, nor shall I give any," made Blackbeard dance with fury.

The pirate chief seized some hand grenades made of empty rum bottles filled with powder and shot, set alight the short fuses and hurled them onto the deck of Maynard's ship.

Although they did no harm, clouds of choking smoke blotted out their sight of the enemy for a few minutes.

Blackbeard seized his chance.

"Jump!" he roared. "Cut them to pieces!"

He led fourteen ruffians aboard the small sloop, shouting and cursing and hacking their way across the decks with great bladed cutlasses.

Blackbeard forced a way aft, advancing in huge lumbering strides, his figure a menacing sight. He swung his cutlass about him, bellowing lustily, and brandished a massive pistol.

Suddenly the smoke drifted away, revealing Blackbeard and Maynard face to face.

Simultaneously their pistols fired and Blackbeard staggered back with a bullet in his chest. But nothing could stop the enraged giant.

He lunged fiercely with his cutlass and both men fought steadily until a sweeping blow from the pirate's cutlass snapped Maynard's blade at the hilt.

A terrible shout burst from Blackbeard, and Maynard faced death as he waited for the final blow from the wildly swinging cutlass. But a British sailor leapt across and caught the pirate a terrific gash across the throat. At the same time a bullet fired by the bo'sun hit him in the side.

The giant figure, streaming blood, eyes glaring wildly to the last, swayed defiantly, then suddenly crashed to the deck.

Blackbeard had fought his last fight.

When they saw their leader fall, the remaining pirates lost heart and jumped overboard, or begged for mercy. This was granted and they were hauled out of the water to be put in chains on Maynard's ship.

Meanwhile his other sloop, after hastily repairing the damage caused by Blackbeard's shot, came up and captured the crew still aboard Blackbeard's ship.

Blackbeard's fierce, grinning head was then lopped off his body and hung from the bowsprit of Maynard's sloop.

Thirteen of the prisoners were hanged in Virginia after trial. Israel Hands, ashore at the time of battle, was also condemned to die, but the timely arrival of a Proclamation prolonging the King's Pardon for piracy saved him.

Provided with documents which were found on Blackbeard's ship and which incriminated Eden and Knight, Maynard seized the sugar that had been their share of the loot from the Martinique prize.

A board of enquiry was set up to investigate the business dealings which Eden and Knight had had with Blackbeard, but their luck seems to have held since no decisions were ever reached.

Maynard's battered sloop sailed into Bath with its gruesome figurehead, and as news of the pirate's death swept round the relief and excitement of the people was tremendous.

Maynard was the hero of the day.

As the years went by, romance glorified the story of Blackbeard and he became a legend—a fantastic figure of devilish ferocity whose awful deeds ranked him with the fearful Attila the Hun.

Some of the stories told about him are true, some are magnified into legends. Yet however incredible some of them may sound, there is no doubt that most of them are based upon true events.

Not knowing fear himself, he was feared by all his men whom he ruled with a hand of iron.

7
The City of Sin

Thundering down the western coast of Central America one day in 1692, a mighty earthquake brought the avenging fury of Nemesis to the most sinful city that the hands of man have ever erected: Port Royal, "cesspool of Christendom."

For years the pirate stronghold on the island of Jamaica was a safe haven in which the sea-wolves defied what law there was and indulged in every vice that the human brain could invent.

From this hideout corsairs of all nationalities set out in search of plunder, and to its safety they returned with their ill-gotten booty.

Port Royal was a city of many tongues. Swashbuckling cutthroats with scarred faces and gold rings dangling from their ears, roistering fierce-whiskered brigands with cutlasses and pistols in their sashes and bracelets around the wrists, merchants in full-skirted coats and cocked hats, all jostled along the waterfront where sloops and ketches, galleys and craft of all kinds lay at anchor. There was always the tang of rope and canvas and tobacco smoke in the heat-laden air.

Vice and corruption flourished. Fortunes were made and lost in the gambling dens; and when all was gone men went to sea again.

Few there were who did not believe that divine judgment swept Port Royal into the sea that fateful day, and certainly the place deserved it.

Here were gathered the lowest of the low: sweepings from the slums and prisons of Europe who came to spend the loot that they had wrested from Spanish plate ships and any others unfortunate enough to cross their path.

Life for the pirates of the Caribbean was hard and inclined to be short; but in Port Royal they could give full reign to all the desires of their wolfish natures.

Here they could buy slave girls of many races, from Indian maidens to captured senoritas, and watch almost unbelievable forms of entertainment in theatres.

A popular sport was "sparrow shooting," the target being a slave or captured Spaniard fastened to a stake by a long chain which gave him freedom to jump about trying to dodge the pistol balls fired from a distance. Each part of the body was worth so many points if hit.

Highly organized, the pirates ran their island in similar fashion to that of the Brethren on Tortuga. Laws were drawn up with penalties for breaking them. There was even a sort of welfare state which gave a fixed sum from common funds to pirates who lost limbs or became totally unfit through injuries received in action.

The wealthier pirate chiefs who had gathered enough plunder often retired to live the life of landed gentry. They set up sugar mills, plantations, distilleries and built themselves some of the finest mansions in the whole of the New World.

Such was the sea gangsters' kingdom. Its coast-line bristling with cannon it was impregnable to anything but a very large fleet. The Spanish, fully occupied with convoying their precious plate ships and guarding the scattered outposts of an empire too big to handle, never found time to raise such a fleet.

England, her sea dogs often no better than legalized pirates challenging the might of Spain in the New World, tended to smile upon this hornets' nest that wreaked such havoc among the ships and possessions of the hated Don.

But the gods were less tolerant. . . .

That last dawn came hot and sullen. Far away beneath the ocean bed a part of the earth's surface buckled and from the depths a vast wall of water surged up, shattering like matchboxes the little ships of men that it encountered, sweeping across islands and leaving them bare and clean.

In the path of the roaring wave stood Port Royal. . . .

The revellers from last night's orgy lay in drunken stupor, some of them in the streets.

The first they knew that the day of judgment had come was when a mighty wind came blasting inshore, striking the town like the lash of a whip, tearing off roofs and bending the palms.

Terror-stricken, the inhabitants fled for the shelter of stone buildings, but no place was safe.

Soon, tremors shook the ground, and screaming humans tumbled into the great cracks that opened. Then came the wave, driving before it the ships in the bay and smashing them into the town.

For a few minutes the water covered everything. When it went Port Royal was nowhere to be seen. An evil blot had been washed from the face of the earth. No more than a few dozen people survived.

There is a legend in Jamaica today; the locals say that on still nights you can hear the bells of the cathedral tolling from the bottom of the bay—rung by the unquiet souls of the wolves of the Spanish Main.

8
"Gentlemen" Pirates

Piracy as a profession seems to have attracted certain men of good breeding, culture and education; and that is something of a mystery. Why should a career of danger, hardship and lawlessness have had such an appeal?

Some, perhaps, just tired of conventional life and craved adventure. Others fell for the lure of gold on a scale which an ordinary hum-drum life could never provide.

The ranks of the corsairs contain all manner of men—strange, inscrutable characters ranging from sons of noble families to lawyers, soldiers and churchmen.

"Why stay at home, man? Come sail with me on the Spanish Main. Feel the sun on your face, hear the wind in the rigging of a tall ship with the skull and crossbones at your mast!"

Many there were, trapped behind office desks in the crowded, disease-ridden cities of Europe who heard those words from friends returned with rich prizes.

"There's treasure on those seas for the taking: the galleons of the Dons loaded with gold and silver plate from the land of the Incas; and rich towns along the coasts to be burned and looted. And when you come home rich you can buy a fine house, or settle where the sun is warm with servants and fine carriages."

So they listened to the voices of temptation, to those

tales of the apparent ease with which vast profits could be made, of the merchants who were in the market to buy bales of wool and silk, casks of wine and brandy, pearls and ambergris and gold and silver without asking awkward questions.

And some of them fell for the siren voices and sailed for that New World of adventure beyond the western horizon. The dream turned out to be real—for a few; but many there were who came back legless or armless after an encounter with a red-hot cannon ball hurtling through the air, or perhaps because they were a little too slow to avoid the swing of a cutlass.

Others never did come back. Their bodies fed the sharks in the Caribbean, or rotted in tropical jungles along the Isthmus of Panama, or swung in the western wind on the end of a gallows rope.

Right and wrong differ from one period to another, even from one country to another; and in the sixteenth and seventeenth centuries the concept of right and wrong was often very different from ours.

Piracy was looked upon almost as a gentlemanly profession rather than a crime; and the dividing line between a licensed privateer charged with attacking only the King's enemies, and a freebooter who did not bother with such distinctions or with legal permits was often very thin.

LANCELOT BLACKBURNE was one of the strangest characters in the annals of piracy. An Oxford scholar he roamed the Caribbean for several years as a member of a pirate crew, then returned to become Archbishop of York!

THOMAS LODGE, son of a Lord Mayor of London and educated at Trinity College, Oxford; Doctor of Physics and a poet, threw up a brilliant career to join the "Brethren of the Main."

ENDYMION PORTER was a protege of Charles I and Gentleman of the King's Bedchamber who combined diplomacy with occasional piratical exploits, sometimes, so it was rumored, with the approval of his royal master.

MAJOR STEDE BONNET's is one of the strangest cases. A soldier who came from a line of distinguished army men he turned pirate for no apparent reason. Who can say why this retired officer and owner of rich estates on Barbados cut himself loose from friends and the ordinary life to which he was accustomed? Was it for a few short years of excitement and adventure that he took the step which led him to the gallows?

THOMAS LODGE M.D. was not related to the Thomas Lodge of Oxford. This one was a Cambridge scholar and respected medical man. When almost fifty he invested his life savings in a privateering venture.

The organizers were Captain Woodes Rogers and William Dampier, and it was with them that Lodge helped to rescue from the lonely island of Juan Fernandez the Scottish sailor on whose adventures Daniel Defoe based his novel *Robinson Crusoe*.

Later, cruising along the coast of Honduras they came to the town of Guayaquil which they attacked with cannon shot.

Surprised that there was no reaction they landed and found the town deserted. After a few hours they found a heap of corpses in one of the churches, and recognised to their horror victims of the plague. Soon the crew themselves were stricken down with the fearsome disease and two-thirds of them died. It was due to Lodge's care and treatment that the rest survived.

A portrait of dreaded buccaneer Henry Morgan.

Henry Morgan. Shown here at Panama when he sacked the city and loaded its wealth onto his ships. (*See Chapter 1*)

Morgan's invasion and total destruction of the fortified town of Puerto del Principe, which he ransacked, sailing to Jamaica with a load of more than £1 million.

Spanish galleons destroyed by Morgan.

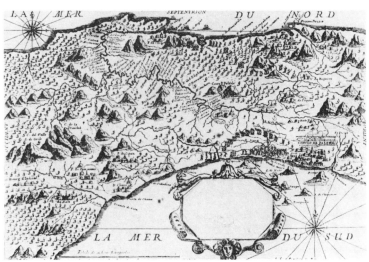

An old map of the Isthmus of Panama.

Blackbeard. (See Chapter 6)

The death of Blackbeard.

Pirates sinking buried treasure. (*See Chapter 9*)

Pirate burying treasure.

Pirates burying treasure.

Ruins of church in old Panama, where pirate gold has been discovered.

Anne Bonney. (See Chapter 10)

Mary Read. (See Chapter 10)

Thomas Lodge M.D. was one of the lucky pirates. After three successful years he returned to Bristol and his job as a doctor. He wrote books on hygiene and general health and one of his prescriptions, *Dover's Powder,* still remains in use as a remedy for gout.

HENRY SIMMS, an old Etonian turned pirate came of good family but was expelled from college for "inclinations to vice." His father bought him a share in a breechmaker's business but Henry ran away. When next heard of he was in prison as a pickpocket and later deported to New England.

He joined an English merchantman which was captured by pirates. Henry threw in with them but turned out to be a very inefficient pirate. He roamed the West Indies for some time but without taking any rich prizes.

Disillusioned, he took advantage of a royal amnesty and next turned up in Bristol where he bought a horse and pistol and tried his hand at being a highwayman; but he was no more successful at this than at piracy. He was soon caught and hanged.

LE SIEUR RAVANAU DE LUSSON was one of the most colorful of all the filibusters. Descendant of a noble French family he was of an aristocratic appearance with all the manners of a gentleman.

His stirring life reads like a romantic tale. Used to a life of ease and luxury he gambled away his inheritance and found himself surrounded by creditors. To refill his empty purse he fled to the Caribbean and joined a pirate ship. His exploits soon extended even to the Pacific and all along the coast from Panama down to Peru; but unlike many he was neither villain nor scoundrel.

Chivalrous and religious he strictly forbade his men to molest priests or rob churches; and before plundering a town his men had to attend Mass with him. Also he never permitted torture. Often he ran a "protection racket" by promising to protect wealthy churches in return for payment.

The pirate aristocrat eventually returned to France laden with treasure and settled down in Paris as a respected gentleman of fashion.

Such were a few of those who sought fortune with the skull and crossbones for their flag.

9
Where to Seek Hidden Treasure

Where should you look for buried treasure?

According to an old lady who appeared on television with me some years ago, you should search in the China Sea. There, she claimed, the famous pirate, Captain Kidd, hid a huge fortune. She produced an old, yellowing chart on which was marked the exact spot where the treasure was to be found. She had worked for a Bournemouth solicitor, who had left her a collection of sea chests and daggers, and flags bearing the once dreaded skull and crossbones. Included in the collection was an ancient bureau which she was sure had belonged to Kidd. And it was in a secret compartment of that bureau that the chart had been found.

As the treasure was said to be worth £2 million, arrangements were being made to send out an expedition to recover the treasure. As a matter of fact, her chart prompted the formation of two expeditions, neither of which found any of the treasure. Nor was the American expedition which, at the same time, was ransacking Oak Island, thousands of miles away, in search of the same treasure. Which is hardly surprising, as it is very doubtful that William Kidd was ever a pirate, and so it is very improbable that he ever had any plunder to bury.

There is, however, a good deal of convincing evidence that treasure does lie buried in various parts of the world.

And the prospect of tracking down such treasure has tempted men—yes, and also women—to spend a great deal of time and often all their money looking for it. Unfortunately, most of the ventures have failed. Even those who succeeded in locating the supposed hiding places found that others had been there before them, taking away whatever loot they had discovered.

The seeker for treasure might well look to the West Indies, and particularly to Tortuga, which is a small island northwest of Hispaniola. Hundreds of the islands in the West Indies were favorite resorts of pirates, as they offered ideal hideouts for men who were cutthroats and robbers on the largest scale, and who needed to keep clear of the law.

In 1687, Sir William Phips, Governor of Massachusetts, recovered from a Spanish plateship sunk off the coast of Hispaniola gold and silver worth £300,000. But this large amount is believed to be only half of the valuables that went down with the ship. Phips was forced by bad weather to abandon his search, and when he returned, a few months later, it was to learn that news of his find had attracted many adventurers to the wreck. They had made off with the treasure he had been forced to leave behind.

In 1671, Henry Morgan—one of the greatest of all Welsh adventurers and a man of incredible daring and imagination—attacked Old Panama. This Spanish city was a vast storehouse in which were hidden large quantities of gold and silver, brought there by mule trains from the mines of Peru and other provinces. It was stored there until it could be shipped to Spain in her many galleons. A fleet of these made the hazardous Atlantic crossing twice a year.

When Morgan sacked Old Panama, the inhabitants set fire to it, but gold, silver and diamonds do not burn, and the Welshman and his pirates uncovered a great deal of loot. But they did not find it all, and it is known that the inhabitants hid away most of their wealth before fleeing into the jungle. They secreted their jewels and precious metals in underground tunnels and vaults, and in the three hundred years that have passed since the town was sacked, the ruins have become overgrown with thick bush and trees.

Old Panama, however, has by no means been neglected. It has been visited countless times by treasure seekers. Again and again the ground has been combed and quartered, without the seekers finding anything of great value. But an Englishman did make a sensational find after the First World War. He unearthed several gold and silver cups, plus a large ball of solid gold which, experts believe, formed part of a life size statue of the Virgin Mary.

The lure of buried treasure has as strong an appeal as ever. This explains why Cocos Island, 300 miles off the coast of Costa Rica, is still visited by treasure-seeking expeditions. This island is no more than three square miles in all, and it has been searched again and again by men who knew how to be thorough in their seeking. Yet not so much as one doubloon has been found there. Nevertheless, such is the attraction of wealth hidden and waiting to be unearthed, that a Captain Brinkinghorn organized a syndicate of seekers in the 1920s. A retired mariner, no doubt he felt he had the experience to equip him for such an undertaking. But it came to nothing.

This is surprising, as it has never been seriously disputed that at least three pirate hoards were buried on

Cocos Island in the days when robbery at sea was regarded as something of an international pastime. Of the three lots of loot, that hidden by Captain Thompson is thought to be faraway the most valuable. When Simon Bolivar, the famous South American Liberator, was freeing the New World from Spanish tyranny, he took Lima amongst many other towns and cities. Before he reached Lima, the citizens chartered William Thompson's brig, the *Mary Dean,* to carry them and their wealth to Callao. In this they made a grave mistake, for their wealth amounted to some £4 million, a fortune Thompson decided to make his own. Having drowned all his passengers, he made for Cocos Island. There he hid the booty in a cave, intending to return for it later.

He went to Newfoundland, where he became mortally ill. Before he died, he revealed to a friend called Keating the secret of the treasure he had left on Cocos Island. Keating visited the island several times, always returning with a quantity of gold coins. This drew increasing attention to his expeditions, and he decided it would be prudent to abandon them. Whether this saved him from being murdered by those determined to share the Thompson hoard is not known, for the end of his life remains a mystery.

The other two hoards of treasure, which all the evidence indicates were hidden on the island, were taken there by Captain Edward Davis in 1683, and by the Portuguese pirate, Bonito Benito, in 1819. They were said to be made up of several tons of gold bullion, barrels crammed with gold and silver coins and jewel-studded church ornaments. In the years that followed the island attracted treasure seekers of many nationalities, yet not one could claim to have found so much as a silver dollar, although they examined the island inch by inch.

A recent English expedition was led by none other than the late Sir Malcolm Campbell. Equipped with old maps and modern mining tools, they spent several weeks examining the sea-caves with which the cliffs are honeycombed. But they fared no better than those who had been there before them.

Nevertheless, the existence of the "Cocos Island Treasure" is officially confirmed in the British Foreign Office handbook issued for 1935. This states that it is known that the treasure consists of 350 tons of bullion, 300,000 pounds weight of silver, 733 bars of gold and seven kegs of gold coin. Strange indeed that so much should be so well hidden in such a small space.

There has been no more success in the search for the treasure said to be buried on Oak Island. Many individuals have spent months on this uninhabited island looking for the wealth thought to be stored there. Amongst several bodies which have searched the island was an American syndicate which sank 60,000 dollars in their enterprise. It is estimated that a third of a million dollars have been spent in digging up Oak Island, and all for nothing at all.

Buried treasure, in fact, except in rare cases, has the strange and frustrating quality of remaining buried.

10
Deadlier than the Male: A Trio of Bloodthirsty Wenches

In the Public Record Office at Spanish Town, known in former times as St. Iago de la Vega, Jamaica, there is preserved a rare and quaintly worded record, entitled—

> The TRYALS of Captain John Rackham, and other PIRATES who were all condemn'd for PIRACY, at the Town of St. Iago de la Vega, in the island of JAMAICA, on Wednesday and Thursday the Sixteenth and Seventeenth Days of November 1720, as also the TRYALS of Mary Read and Anne Bonney who were also condemn'd for "PIRACY."

Lurid as are the chronicles of sea-robbers who followed the cult of the Black Flag in the heyday of buccaneering, for sheer devilry they pale beside the deeds of some of the women pirates of the early eighteenth century whose audacious exploits add a highly colored page to piratical romance.

Making all allowance for the probability that, in the passage of time, such tales have acquired an historical patina, their glamor makes them irresistible to such of us, who, by force of convention and circumstances, must be content to indulge any subconscious leanings to lawless adventure, at second hand, or equally to those who merely like to be thrilled.

Whether or not women number largely in the great

company of readers of this class of literature is a matter for conjecture but that members of "the weaker sex" have, in the past, and right up into recent times, carried out the business of robbery by violence on the high seas and inland waters with conspicuous success, is irrefutable.

Outshining the fiercest of these sanguinary ladies who followed the profession are Anne Bonney, Mary Read and Maria Cobham. Each was drawn from a different social background and their lives have been filled with amazing adventures that make stranger reading than the wildest fiction.

Take the case of Anne Bonney, daughter of a notary or solicitor, practicing in County Cork, Ireland. There was nothing in her antecedents to account for her latent propensities. Anne was a pretty, vivacious child, idolized by her father, who, until his liaison with his wife's maid came to light with the birth of Anne, had a good standing in local professional circles, but the gradual decline in prestige and revenue brought about a determination to emigrate, and take the child with him, to America, to try his luck there. Shortly after their arrival he changed his legal profession for that of a planter and Anne grew to attractive girlhood in the pleasant setting of a comfortable home in Carolina where her father had become a prosperous estate owner. The old man had ambitious plans for Anne's future, who kept house for him until she reached the age of sixteen, but these plans were brought to an abrupt termination when the girl announced that she had fallen in love with a good-looking but penniless sailor whom she had met and whom she was going to marry. She would not listen to her father's earnest entreaties to give up this mad plan, and being headstrong and possessing a violent temper, she eloped with her betrothed, whereupon the irate parent refused to sanction the match and cut Anne off with the proverbial shilling.

A bride with expensive tastes and no money was not to the bridegroom's liking, who had expected that his young wife would be well provided for by her father. Finding that her only fortune was her good looks and having no means to support himself and his wife, the pair sailed to the island of New Providence in the Bahamas, where he hoped to find employment. In the early eighteenth century this group of islands was one of the favorable "resting" places of the Caribbean pirates and buccaneers who retired there in the intervals between their nefarious exploits, and a more villainous riffraff of cutthroats it would have been hard to find. In this setting, then, appeared handsome John Rackham, famed and feared throughout the West Indies for his daredevil acts of piracy. He met Anne and swept her off her feet, and there started an alliance which carried her straight on to the stage where she was to play out her life's drama. Anne asked her sailor husband that he should give her her freedom in exchange for a liberal sum of money which her new, dashing lover offered to provide. As this proposal was indignantly refused, Anne jumped at Rackham's suggestion that she should go to sea with him in his ship, disguised in man's clothes, pledging herself that she would not reveal the secret of her sex to her shipmates.

Anne accompanied her pirate-lover on all his buccaneering cruises and eventually proved to be his equal with sword and pistol and his superior in audacity and reckless courage. She fought, pillaged and plundered with ruthless brutality, her only concession to her womanhood being an occasional retirement when a child was born to her. On these occasions she usually stayed in Cuba, living in the extravagance and luxury characteristic of the successful freebooter.

Whenever these incidents were over, Anne joined Rackham again, sailing under the skull and crossbones, and acting as his trusted lieutenant. Before the curtain was finally rung down on the amazing career of this sea-amazon, fate played one of those strange tricks which writers of fiction would be hesitant to introduce into the plots of their stories. It was on the deck of the very brigantine on which Anne sailed with her lover that another woman, also disguised in man's clothes, made a dramatic entrance.

So complete was the appearance of both that each took the other for what she appeared to be. In many ways the life of Mary Read in her early womanhood had been singularly like that of Anne Bonney, as will be seen later. Mary's fair skin and beardless face gave her a boyish appearance, and her fine, sparkling eyes and cheerful manners were a challenge to Anne's susceptibilities. Unaware of each other's secret, Anne took an immediate liking to the dashing "young man" and finally confessed to Mary that she had fallen in love with her, revealing at the same time her sex, much to the latter's embarrassment. Under the circumstances Mary had no choice but in turn to divulge her womanhood, also. After the amorous Anne had recovered from her surprise and, it may be assumed, disappointment, the two girls became close friends. Rackham was greatly disturbed by the growing intimacy between his sweetheart and the young sailor and in a fit of violent jealousy threatened that he would cut the young man's throat. Therefore, to quiet her irate lover Anne was forced to let him into the secret, which Rackham never betrayed.

The recorded history of Mary Read suggests that her early environment, unlike that of Anne Bonney, may have had some influence in the shaping of her chosen career. Her mother, who seems to have had no scruples where self-interest was affected, was the wife of a merchant skipper and Mary was born during one of the voyages on which Mrs. Read usually accompanied her husband. For the first few years of her life the girl lived on board her father's ship and it is therefore little wonder that the sea was in her blood.

Mary had a brother, one year older than herself, and when her father died her mother set up home with the children in a small Devonshire village where she appears to have supported herself and son and daughter by her wits rather than by hard work. Her late husband's mother who lived in Plymouth was fairly well-to-do and it was presumed that her grandson might expect to be her heir but he, unfortunately, died shortly after the family had settled down. But Mary's mother had no intention to let a trifle such as this stand in the way of an inheritance, and conceived the bold plan that her daughter must cease to exist as a girl and must forthwith impersonate her dead brother. By dressing her in his clothes and coaching her in the ways of little boys Mary turned out to be a most apt pupil and entered enthusiastically into the spirit of what was to her mind an exciting adventure.

The ruse was entirely successful and when Mrs. Read presented her daughter to the old lady, who had never seen her grandson before, she was completely deceived. She was delighted with the bright and handsome "lad" and did not question his genuineness for one single moment. So pleased, indeed, was she, that she contributed a small sum each week towards "his" support.

However, when Mary was thirteen the grandmother died and despite all schemes and machinations it was discovered that she had left her money elsewhere and her "grandson" did not profit by a penny.

The girl continued masquerading and living as a boy and, when the time came to earn her living, a job as a pageboy at a small hotel was found for her. But Mary quickly tired of the monotony of the work and the restrictions it imposed upon her mercurial nature and obtained employment at one of the dockside taverns where she felt more at ease among the sailors and longshoremen who frequented them. Yet, her roving spirit would not let her rest and she ran away to sea, enlisting in the Queen's Navy and serving as a "powder monkey" on board a man-of-war. After a few years' service she became fed up with the hard life and, when the ship was at anchor at a Flemish port, deserted and joined a foot regiment as a cadet, or volunteer. She fought with daring and bravery in several actions and her courage and gallantry won her the notice and good opinion of her officers and comrades. To her disappointment, however, she was not promoted, in spite of her fine record, whereupon she quitted the service in disgust and enlisted in a cavalry regiment.

By this time Mary had grown into a dashing creature, lithe and supple of figure and with merry, laughing eyes. Fighting, swearing and drinking with the best of them, her high spirits soon made her a favorite among her messmates, none of whom ever suspected that the good-looking lad was in reality a woman. Fate, however, challenged her in the person of a handsome young cavalryman who joined the band with her and with whom she fell violently in love. To him she revealed the secret of her sex and the two lovers became inseparable companions.

When the campaign was drawing to a close and the regiment had gone into winter quarters Mary publicly made a clean breast of the situation, much to the amazement and delight of her comrades, and, for the first time since early babyhood, appeared dressed as a woman. Shortly afterwards the pair were married and the unusual circumstances so intrigued the commanding officer that he and his staff not only assisted at the marriage ceremony but made a gift of money to bride and groom. Mary and her husband then obtained their discharge and settled down at Breda where they opened a tavern, or eating house, at the sign of the "Three Horseshoes." Owing to the romantic nature of their adventurous past the young couple soon did a thriving business and numbered among their guests many of their former officers as well as not a few of the wealthy burghers of the town.

After a while, Mary's husband fell ill and died soon afterwards, which brought the one and only domestic interlude in Mary's life to a close. With the coming of the Peace of Ryswick most of the soldiery whose patronage of the tavern had proved so lucrative disbanded and trade decreased so rapidly that Mary was forced to sell out. But she had by no means sown all the wild oats of which she was capable and, deciding to become a young man once again, donned male attire and went back to army life, joining a regiment of foot garrisoned in one of the Dutch seaport towns. As was to be expected, after a life of independence spent in comparative luxury and having been made much of by her former associates Mary revolted against the strict military discipline and made up her mind to go to sea again. She watched her opportunity and when a Dutch West Indiaman was on the point of leaving port, she deserted and joined its crew.

The journey was uneventful until the Island of New Providence or the Bahamas, as they are now known, was almost sighted, when the vessel was assailed and seized by English pirates who ransacked it, but set the crew free and let them continue their journey with the exception of Mary, who was the only English sailor on board. Having been greatly impressed by her cool-headed behavior during the action they forced her to throw in her lot with them. For some time Mary sailed under the Black Flag, taking to the adventurous life as a duck takes to water and handling cutlass and pistol like any man; nobody ever realized she was a girl.

The Bahamas were at that time one of the resorts of pirates under the main leadership of Van and Edward Teach, the infamous "Blackbeard," and their daring sea-robberies had become so intolerable that Captain Woodes Rogers was sent there by the British Government, charged to suppress piracy and stamp out the evils by every means at his disposal including persuasive charm—which he possessed in no small degree—the offer of a free pardon to all those pirates who surrendered by a given date, and by armed force to bring the recalcitrants to justice. Captain Rogers was the famous navigator who, nine years earlier, rescued Alexander Selkirk, the hero of "Robinson Crusoe's Island" while on an expedition against the Spaniards at Guayaquil. So well did he succeed through his commanding personality, no less than through his strategy, that not only did many of the pirates and buccaneers, who some reports claim to have numbered well over two thousand, surrender and receive their pardon but actually helped Captain Rogers with the trial and execution of some of those of their former companions in crime who reverted and were recaptured.

The crew of the pirate ship which captured the Dutch Indiaman had put into Nassau on New Providence Island and settled ashore. Mary among them. She lived there quietly when Captain Rogers arrived with his free pardon to all pirates, in 1718, but her money began to grow short and hearing of a privateering expedition being sent out by Captain Rogers to cruise against the Spaniards, Mary signed on as a member of the crew, which consisted in the main of converted freebooters.

The ship had hardly left port when these men mutinied, deciding to return to their old calling. They put the captain into irons and elected one of their number, John Rackham, as their leader. This man was a powerful, swashbuckling blackguard, nicknamed "Calico Jack," whose exploits as a seasoned member of the infamous "Brethren of the Coast" had earned him a sinister reputation. One of the first to express their willingness to sign on under pirate regulations was Mary. This, at last, she felt, was her opportunity to lead the kind of life for which she was really fitted and Rackham had no objection to adding the lively, courageous "lad" to his company.

Fate was ready to take a hand in shaping Mary's destiny. To her unbounded astonishment she was confronted on board by Anne Bonney, pattern of all women brigands, who always sailed with her sweetheart, John Rackham, wearing men's clothes, the same as Mary did.

For some turbulent months Rackham sailed the main taking and looting several merchantmen homeward bound from Jamaica. In one of these successful raids an attractive youth with engaging manners was taken prisoner to whom Mary lost her heart. No doubt, this was the main reason why Mary did not fasten her affection on the captain resulting in amicable relations between the two women being maintained, and why no jealousy or rivalry arose between them. On the contrary, they fought valiantly side by side, using sword and musketoon with terrorizing effect on their victims.

In the course of the cruise Mary proved her devotion to her lover by an act of stoical heroism. Her sweetheart quarreled violently with a fellow pirate who challenged him to a duel. As the sloop lay at anchor at one of the islands the men appointed an hour for the following day when they would go ashore and fight. Desperate in her anxiety that the man whom she loved might be killed, Mary picked a quarrel with the fellow challenging him to a duel herself, the latter agreeing to fight it two hours earlier than his engagement with his other opponent. Unknown to her lover the two antagonists went ashore at the appointed time and both fighting with sword and pistol alike, in true pirate fashion, Mary outwitted the ferociously attacking ruffian by taking him off his guard and wounding him mortally.

For some time fortune was kind to Jack Rackham and several merchantmen were captured. But as was usual in a sea-robber's career, retribution overtook him. A big fast-sailing sloop which had been sent out by the Governor of Jamaica, manned by a detachment of marines, sighted the pirate ship and went at once in pursuit of it. Before the more cumbersome brigantine's anchor was weighed the sloop came up and the King's men boarded it.

In the ensuing skirmish none of the pirates, with the exception of Mary Read and Anne Bonney and one of the crew, kept the deck. All the others, including the captain, fled below deck in panic, upon which the two women ran after them and, cursing them as cowards, forced them at pistol's point to come up again and fight like men. However, the odds were heavy against the demoralized pirate crew and the only three who had shown courage and valor realized the hopelessness of their plight and surrendered.

All the prisoners were taken to Jamaica where Jack and his followers were given a quick trial and sentenced to be hanged. Rackham was executed at Gallows Point, Port Royal and his body was later cut down and hung in chains on one of the quays, along with eight of his crew. Mary and Anne managed each to escape vengeance. As they were found to be expectant mothers at the time of their trials, execution was postponed but Mary died in prison of a fever at the age of only 27 years. Anne was reprieved after the birth of a child but no record can be found of what eventually became of her.

The last request of Rackham to be allowed to visit his sweetheart before his execution was granted as a special favor but it brought him instead of consolation, sneering taunts from the outraged Anne, whose parting words to him were: "I am sorry to see you here, Jack, but if you had fought like a man you would not now be hanged like a dog."

The last of the trio, Maria Cobham, was apparently of an even more diabolical disposition than many of her male accomplices. Little is known of her antecedents but she probably frequented the quayside taverns of Plymouth and met there young Cobham, a smuggler from Poole turned pirate, who picked her up when he landed after raiding his first big ship off the Mersey. She was an Indiaman, which he boarded, scudding her and drowning the entire crew, carrying off booty worth no less than £40,000. Recognizing a kindred spirit in Maria Cobham, he induced her to accompany him in his next expedition. She proved to be an apt pupil, and although she must have had something of a dual personality, this was no drawback, for she gained the allegiance of the pirate crew by interceding with Captain Cobham to lighten their punishment when he had imposed drastic penalties for some misdoings. Yet this same woman took a fiendish delight devising ways of torture for captives, none of whom received any mercy. Cobham's pleasant way of liquidating his unfortunate victims after having scuttled their ship was to tie them alive in sacks and throw them overboard. Maria added the spice of refinement to the proceedings by prolonging their agony. She indulged in acts of refined cruelties, reserving to herself the despatching of the ship's officers, one of her favorite methods being to truss them up to a support and then use them as targets, shooting or stabbing them to slow death.

Beneath all her savagery Maria nursed social ambitions; she set her heart on becoming chatelaine of a large establishment, coveting possession of a beautiful place at Poole in Dorset, her husband having come from this port. With this end in view, she dissuaded Captain Cobham from retiring when he would have wished to do so but, having made a large fortune, he eventually gave up piracy. Maria's last act of villainy was as black as the flag under which she had put to sea—poisoning the whole crew of an Indiaman which the pirates had taken. Cobham purchased a large estate at Havre complete with private harbor and a pleasure yacht in which the pair and a crew of former associates went out on fishing expeditions. One day they encountered a merchant ship which lay becalmed off the coast and the temptation to seize it became too strong for the ex-pirates. They boarded the brig, shot the captain and crew and carried the prize to Bordeaux, where they sold the vessel. After this final episode Cobham and Maria settled down to live in palatial style on their vast, ill-gotten fortune. It is a supreme touch of irony that this couple of blackguards whose appalling acts of barbarous cruelties stand unequalled in the bloodstained chronicles of piratical iniquity should not only have escaped punishment but have gained the respect of their neighbors and been treated with deference as people of quality. But such was the case. Indeed, Cobham actually became a justice of the peace famed for his rectitude and condemnation of wrong-doing. At length he died, at a ripe old age, in the sanctity of respectability. Stricken with remorse and haunted by spectres of the grim past, Maria committed suicide by taking poison.

Although one would assume that sea brigandry is now a closed vocation for women, it is well to remember that at least two of them were making a success of it in recent times, the Chinese woman pirate, Mrs. Ching, and her compatriot, Mrs. Hon-Cho-Lo, as late as the nineteen twenties. This young and beautiful widow, who inherited from her husband a pirate junk fleet, decided to carry on the family business. She made herself feared by everybody in the Pathhoi district who had either money or goods to be seized, or a daughter to be kidnapped. She tortured the crews of her prizes or made them walk the plank, then seized the cargo and set fire to the ship.

Her efficiency and brutality, surpassing anything achieved by her late husband, rather points to prove that when woman takes to crime and cruelty she is, indeed, deadlier than the male.

11
"Long Ben": The Colorful Account of Captain John Avery

Among the colorful characters in the history of robbery on the high seas no name has captured the imagination of the public more than that of Captain John Avery, nicknamed "Long Ben."

A Devonshire man, he made his appearance in the last quarter of the seventeenth century when we hear of him for the first time as mate in an English merchantman of 30 guns, a crew of 120 men and plenty of stores and provisions. The vessel was the *Duke,* hired by Spain which was at that time at war with France.

The history of John Avery's stirring life reads like a fairy story and rumors about him were whispered throughout European cities almost from the very start of his career until his death in obscurity.

Among the legends woven around him were tales that he had captured and married the beautiful and fabulously rich daughter of an Indian prince, that he was living on the island of Madagascar in royal state and oriental splendor surrounded by a harem of native women and commanding a fleet of fast sloops that took terrible toll of all island shipping.

There is really no evidence to support these highly colored tales. Far from spending a life of luxury and comfort he was driven from pillar to post in trying to sell his ill-gotten plunder and he died penniless in a Devon village, where his body lies in a pauper's grave.

This is John Avery's story. . . .

During the *Duke*'s voyage the wily mate had carefully sounded his shipmates and incited them to mutiny. One night, off a Spanish port, Avery seized the vessel and silently steered her out of the harbor under cover of darkness.

This all happened while the captain of the *Duke* was lying drunk in his cabin where Avery coolly informed him that he had taken over the ship.

He gave the captain the choice of joining the rebellious crew or being cast adrift. The captain chose to be cast off and accompanied by six loyal members of the crew eventually reached shore safely.

The *Duke* proceeded on its journey to Madagascar where Avery hoped to obtain news of the movement of merchant vessels which he might seize.

On arriving at the northeast coast of the island he found two armed sloops at anchor which he took and whose crews joined him willingly on finding that they were brother pirates.

Avery put twelve of his most trusted men on board the sloops to prevent any attempts at trickery on the part of his as yet untried companions and set sail for the Red Sea, which he considered a safe hunting ground for prizes, as England at that time was fully occupied in her war with France and had no ships patrolling that part of the world.

Near the mouth of the river Indus a great tall-masted ship was sighted which proved to be the *Rampura,* belonging to the Great Mogul of India, the most powerful ruler in the East.

When the pirates chased her and unfurled the dreaded Black Flag, the vessel surrendered without putting up any fight.

On boarding, it was found that she was bound on a pilgrimage to Mecca and that she carried no arms.

Among the passengers were two daughters of the Great Mogul, some officers of his court and a number of wealthy merchants, all of whom were treated with courtesy and later put ashore after they had been stripped of everything they owned.

The loot taken from the *Rampura* was believed to be the most fabulous ever recorded. It consisted of a hundred thousand pieces of eight and lavish provisions of all kinds. There were priceless gold and silver goblets, pearl-studded clasps and brooches, armlets and bracelets, silver trays and ivory boxes inlaid with gold, jewelled caskets and perfume in flasks of precious metals.

After the ship had been stripped of all items of value Avery discovered that none of the crew seemed to realize the enormous value of the plundered diamonds and rubies, and that they were well satisfied with their share of the other valuables, which they well knew would realize large sums from Bristol merchants.

Cunningly he hid the larger part of the jewels in a safe place on the *Duke* and invited the captains of the two sloops to visit him.

After entertaining them for some time he pretended to be concerned for the safety of the loot on their vessels and pointed out the hazards they ran if their small sloops were separated by storm or attacked by man-of-war, in which case the whole treasure might be lost.

To provide against such accidents he suggested that it would be wiser to divide the loot into three equal parts, put each into a sealed box and put these into the hold of his own vessel, the much faster and stronger *Duke*. The division could then take place on arrival at Madagascar. The captains agreed to the proposal and went back to their sloops.

Avery now revealed a plan to rob his allies of their share. He pointed out to his crew that there was so much treasure on board the *Duke* that it would make everyone rich and able to live in luxury. All agreed and this piece of treachery was carried out that same night when the *Duke* sneaked away in the darkness and altered course.

It was now decided to head for the American coast where none of them was known and disband there after dividing the treasure.

The *Duke* eventually arrived at the coast of New Providence where Avery sold her with forged documents on the pretense that he was allowed to do so by her owners as she had finished her privateering career. After the three sealed boxes had been opened and the treasure divided the crew parted and went their various ways.

Avery now bought a small sloop and with a few of his remaining companions sailed for Boston where he made a successful deal with the Governor to dispose of the illegal gains. In those days the danger of being convicted for piracy in Boston was slight provided it was made worth while for the authorities to turn a blind eye. It was well known that the Governor was not unfriendly to sea-robbers so long as certain rules of etiquette were followed.

Although Boston merchants were in the market to handle goods which they well knew were stolen, and which included human cargo as well as gold, silver, velvets and brocades, without bothering to inquire about their origin, they fought shy of diamonds and rubies.

We hear of Avery next in Ireland where he went into

hiding. The few of the crew who came with him gave themselves up and were granted the King's Pardon, after which some of them retired into civil life and became respectable tradesmen.

But Avery's efforts to sell the jewels turned out to be as unsuccessful in Ireland as they had been in Boston, and as a court held in his absence had found him guilty of piracy and condemned him to death he felt that Ireland was becoming too hot for him and decided to try his luck in England.

For a while he lived quietly at Bideford in Devonshire under a false name. Through a friend he approached some Bristol merchants who visited him and took away with them the whole of the jewels, leaving him a small sum barely enough for his immediate pressing needs and promising to pay for them as soon as the sale had been completed.

Time dragged on; the little money he had was gone and all pleadings for more were ignored. The merchants laughed, and finally silenced him by threatening to expose him.

The rumors of Avery's marriage to an Indian princess, the great wealth that he was supposed to have enjoyed, the fabled regal state in which he was said to have lived as ruler of a kingdom in Madagascar; all these and other supposed adventures were made the subject of songs and stories and formed the plot for a play called *The Successful Pirate* written by a retired fellow shark of the sea, Captain Charles Johnson.

Avery died destitute and in ill health. Scoundrel though this son of Devon was, it can be said of him that he showed more mercy in his treatment of prisoners than most other pirates.

12
The "Jolly Roger" Flies from the Main Mast

BARTHOLOMEW ROBERTS

By the beginning of the eighteenth century the Elizabethan sea-robbers had degenerated into fully fledged pirates who ravished land and sea regardless of the nationalities of their victims.

Among those sea-wolves was Captain Howel Davis. When he surprised the slave-trader *Princess* off Anamaboa on the Guinea coast and engaged her in combat, her first mate, a Welshman by the name of Bartholomew Roberts, had just finished putting his "black ivory" in irons before weighing anchor when Davis struck.

During the battle Roberts attracted the pirate's attention by his courageous defense and Davis invited him to join up with him.

At first Roberts was not inclined to do so and intended to escape at the first chance. However, it took him only a short time to weigh up the advantages of a relatively guaranteed security against the risks of a life which offered prospects of adventures and the gaining of wealth. He chose the latter.

Davis was killed in a skirmish and Roberts was elected captain in his place. It was decided to sail to the South

American coast and lay in wait there for merchantmen taking rich cargoes to Europe.

Arriving in those waters they cruised about for several weeks when they unexpectedly sighted a Portuguese fleet of 42 vessels anchored off the shore in the bay of Los Todas Santos, apparently waiting to sail for Lisbon. Roberts sailed boldly among them showing the Portuguese colors. To avoid suspicion he ordered most of the crew below deck and steered his course alongside one of the vessels, exchanging greetings with the captain and inviting him on board. He received him most cordially and informed him coolly that it was his intention to attack the treasure ship of the fleet. No harm would come to him if he would point it out and guide him towards her without warning the ship by any signal whatever.

When they came within hail of the vessel which was moored at some distance out of sight of the others, Roberts hauled down the Portuguese flag, hoisted the black bunting on the masthead and opened fire before the surprised captain could muster his crew to man the guns.

A well placed broadside shot her sails to shreds and hit the mainmast which swayed and crashed upon the deck. The ship was now reduced to helplessness and strewn with killed or wounded men when the pirates scaled the bulwarks and pounced upon the deck. After the fight was over the Portuguese was a sinking hull.

Having brought off what deserves to be called one of the most spectacular coups committed by any pirate and loaded with the booty taken, Roberts and his crew retired to a small island in the Surinam River to rest and enjoy the fruits of their ventures in security.

After some weeks of drunken orgies and dissipating

the spoil by gambling and debauchery it was decided to sail north and cruise in the Caribbean. There in rapid succession he captured two sloops and a Spanish galleon out of which he took 130,000 gold coins.

It was in these waters that Roberts met with the only definite defeat in the whole of his piratical career in the course of which he is reputed to have seized or destroyed forty vessels. It happened when the attack on an armed merchantman off Barbados miscarried and the pirates had to retreat.

Roberts was of a commanding appearance. He was tall and his wiry figure towered above his fellows. His face, tanned to a deep mahogany, looked as if it had been carved out of ivory and expressed determination in every line. His dark hair tumbled forward and lay thick over his forehead. He had a mind swift and alert and boundless energy and courage.

There was a twist to his character. Although lawless and unscrupulous in his actions he treated his prisoners with rare leniency, nor did he use force to make his captives join his ranks.

His word was law and every man had to perform the part allotted to him. He was a man of iron will and upheld strict discipline among his ruffianly crew who were generally more drunk than sober. Roberts himself was a teetotaler. He never allowed gambling or women on board.

After an uneventful cruise to the north along the Atlantic seaboard the pirates arrived on the shores of Newfoundland and entered the harbor of Trepassi where a number of fishing barques were at anchor. Roberts ordered their owners to the shore, and being disappointed at finding little to rifle on the barques had them all burned and sunk except one French sloop which he took for his own use, putting some men on board and christening her the *Fortune*.

Having played havoc with the cod-fishery, the pirates left Newfoundland and directed their course back to the West Indies.

By some unfortunate lack of foresight, the *Fortune* had omitted to take on enough provisions before sailing, and as they were growing shorter from day to day and as luck to meet with some ship which could be looted for supplies seemed to have left him, Roberts made for Bartholomew Island. The Governor, believing his tale that they were honest merchantmen, received them hospitably and gave them everything they wanted.

While the pirates stayed for some weeks on the island in idleness, the news reached Roberts that a fleet of merchant vessels carrying loads of ivory and other precious cargo was sailing along the Guinea coast homeward bound. This welcome news decided him to make haste for West African waters, bent upon levying heavy toll on the shipping.

On the way there he cast anchor off Martinique where he committed an act of mean brigandage. It was the usual custom in the port for a ship to hoist a flag to invite the merchants to come out in their sloops and trade with her. When their unarmed vessels came within shooting distance he opened fire on them one by one and forced them to hand their goods over to him.

After this the pirates took up the pursuit of the merchant vessels they were in chase of, overhauled and plundered them and let them go, except a French brigantine whose crew signed the pirates' charter and joined Roberts.

Strengthened in men, he continued his cruise to Sierra Leone. One night the French brigantine stole away secretly and when her loss was discovered in the morning the wind was so much against the *Fortune* that it was not possible to recapture her.

The very same day, however, they fell in to windward with a large ship and let her come close up to them when Roberts hoisted the Jolly Roger and boarded her without much resistance.

He gave the prize the name of *Ranger* and retired to a settlement at the mouth of the Leone river where he heard that the British frigate *Swallow,* commanded by Captain Chaloner Ogle, was on his trail.

Trying to shake their pursuers off, the *Fortune* and the *Ranger* kept out of sight of land for some weeks, but fate was about to overtake the fugitives and cut their infamous practices short. In the course of cruising, provisions had grown short and Roberts was faced with having to put in at Cape Lopez to water and take on fresh supplies.

In the meantime, Captain Ogle had been told by the master of a French ship that Roberts was laying in hiding at Cape Lopez Bay. Without losing time the *Swallow* hastened there and found the pirate ship anchored off shore.

Roberts immediately sent out the *Ranger* for an attack whereupon the *Swallow* turned about and sailed away, pretending that she hoped to escape but at the same time letting the pirate come up with her.

As soon as the *Ranger* had drawn near enough she was greeted with a volley of shot. After the surprised pirates had recovered from their shock they fired back and kept up a running fight at the same time trying to get away. After a grim battle lasting two hours the pirates finally called for quarter.

While Roberts, unaware of the *Ranger*'s fate, awaited the return impatiently, the *Swallow* rounded the Cape and came in sight of the runaway.

Roberts boldly prepared for battle. He knew already that this time there was no loophole for escape and that his fate was sealed.

He resolved to fight to the death and blow up his ship rather than surrender. His men clustered round him determined to defend their lives fighting and when he fell, mortally wounded by a shot through his throat, they threw his corpse into the sea according to orders which he had given them before the battle.

FRANÇOIS L'OLONOIS

"The Torturer"

Silently, the fleet of Indian canoes moved shorewards through the night, paddles dipping evenly and without splash.

Ahead, sleeping and unaware of its perils, lay the rich city of Maracaibo, on the Gulf of Venezuela. The advancing canoes split into two groups, each landing on opposite sides of the fort that guarded the city.

As dawn came—a dawn red as the blood that was soon to flow in the streets of doomed Maracaibo—the men leapt from their canoes and revealed themselves to be, not Indians, but bearded, fearsome pirates armed to the teeth.

As they swarmed into the town, firing a fusilade of musket shots, the shifting mists of morning disclosed eight ships standing in the bay. Horrified watchmen on shore, roused at last but too late, saw the skull and crossbones flying at the masts.

Cannon roared from the ships, the redhot balls blasting into the fort.

François L'Olonois, known as the "Torturer," had struck at one of the richest cities of the New World.

In blood and flame Maracaibo died that day; and on the quayside L'Olonois stood up a row of Spanish prisoners and walked along them, slashing off their heads one by one, pausing each time to lick the blood off his cutlass!

The wealthy churches of the city, festooned with valuable altar ornaments, golden goblets, ivory crucifixes and silver candlesticks were plundered and burnt.

From the smoking ruins rose the screams of rich merchants, tortured to make them reveal the hiding places of their money and treasure.

So fiendish and cruel were the torments invented by the "Torturer," including the slow disjointing of limbs, that some even of his own men, rough and hardened though they were, were often sickened by the hideous spectacle.

This notorious sea-robber had previously come to the West Indies from France as an ordinary seaman, and soon attracted the attention of the Governor of Tortuga, who dabbled in semi-piratical ventures in addition to his official duties. L'Olonois proved useful in carrying out orders which the Governor was not keen to have revealed.

The Governor provided L'Olonois with a sloop in which he attacked several Spanish ships, killing all the officers and crew. After this success the young pirate went plundering ship after ship and carrying the cargo home to Tortuga where his sponsor sold it to merchants at half its real value.

But L'Olonois had more ambitious plans. He joined up with another pirate, Michael de Basco, who had a good knowledge of the movements of Spanish ships, and with a crew of 700 in eight vessels sailed for the great prize of Maracaibo.

After two months of riotous debauchery in the captured city the pirates split up, and L'Olonois began to make his way homeward along the route of the Spanish Plate fleet.

On the third day the look-out man shouted "Ship ahoy!" and L'Olonois gave orders to chase the stranger. With the wind in their favor the pirates steadily gained upon the stately vessel lying deeply in the water and recognized her as a Plate ship.

L'Olonois raised the Spanish colors to deceive her, and by clever maneuvering put himself in a good position from which he opened fire.

The guns flashed and thundered, and in the running fight which followed a lucky shot from the sloop smashed away some of the galleon's guns and carried away her mainmast.

Racing in to close quarters the sea-wolves swarmed into the rigging and reached the deck where vicious hand-to-hand fighting followed until the Spaniards were overwhelmed.

Triumphant, L'Olonois returned laden with the booty from the galleon and vast plunder taken at Maracaibo.

His last exploit was his assault on the coastal cities of Yucatan. He made it known that he planned another raiding expedition and had no difficulty in recruiting another 700 men and a fleet of six ships.

He sailed for Yucatan, pillaging cities and spreading terror on the way; but the success of his Maracaibo venture was not to be repeated.

The company quarrelled and many pirates departed. L'Olonois and those who remained with him continued cruising along the coast of Yucatan when a violent storm arose and separated the ships from each other.

His own vessel was shattered against rocks where L'Olonois and others made a raft from wreckage, and were tossed about on the heavy seas for days until they came to the coast of Darien.

Here, weakened and short of weapons, they were captured and killed by the savage Cuna Indians.

It was the end of one of the most cruel and vicious of all pirates.

THOMAS TEW

In all the bloodstained pages of piratical history the names of Thomas Tew, Long Ben, Avery, Teach, Roberts, L'Olonois stand out. As far as any post mortem ill-fame is concerned, William Kidd may be added, but the possibility nearest the truth is that he was made the scapegoat for deeds which he committed with the consent of interested persons in high places.

In Chapter 11 we have told how Captain Avery betrayed his companions and made off with the whole of the Grand Mogul's treasure. Furious and dismayed, the crews of the two sloops found themselves in a dismal situation, their provisions being too low for the lengthy voyage back to Madagascar.

A council was held and it was decided to moor the two sloops and transfer weapons and other utensils on to the land and camp there, relying on fish and game for maintenance. They had not been settled very long when the *Amity* dropped anchor close to the camp. It turned out to be another pirate vessel under the command of Captain Thomas Tew, who held a commission to take French ships cruising along the west coast of Africa.

However, the captain found it pleasanter to go a-pirating and so, instead of carrying out his commission, he set sail for the Arabian coast with the intention of preying on coastal traders.

He had been cruising only for a short time when the lookout man early one morning sighted a ship on the eastern horizon. Tew at once gave chase and on gaining on the unsuspecting vessel saw her to be an Indian merchantman.

He immediately hoisted the black bunting, whereupon the stranger set all her canvas hoping to escape, but her cumbersome bulk was no match for the pirate's agile sloop and when within cannon shot Tew loosed a broadside which tore her sails to rags and shattered the rudder.

She was now in no condition to resist and on boarding her Tew found in her holds treasures that exceeded his wildest hopes. There were ingots of gold and bars of silver, coffers filled with precious stones, bales of silk and wool and other riches.

With this haul Tew returned to Rhode Island where he bought an estate and intended to retire. But a life of leisure did not suit him and he soon became restless. His spirit longed for fresh adventure and he applied for a new privateering commission to capture French ships. This was refused him but when he offered a bribe of £500 it was granted.

Tew now returned to Madagascar where the French

pirate Misson joined him and they jointly sailed in two ships for the Red Sea.

Here they met one of the Great Mogul's vessels which carried pilgrims to the holy city of Mecca. Meeting with little resistance they captured the ship with the loss of only one of their crew.

Besides a valuable booty of all kinds there were a large number of women on board. Tew selected 100 girls of from twelve to sixteen years and took them back to Libertatia, while he put the older women ashore.

Tew had now amassed a fortune large enough to allow him to retire and return to his home on Rhode Island, there to live a life of luxury.

As the *Amity* needed repair he stayed for a while at Madagascar, living in the Republic of Libertatia as guest of its founder, the French buccaneer Captain Misson.

On his way home round the Cape of Good Hope, Tew captured a Dutch East Indiaman and an English slave trader and arrived safely at Newport, Rhode Island, where he made his peace with his employers in Bermuda by sending them an ample share of loot.

Strange as it may seem, no questions were asked about the legality of Tew's ventures, nor was he taken as a pirate when he set foot on American soil, although his deeds must have been known to the authorities.

Tew settled down and lived quietly for a while at his island home, resisting all requests made by some of his old companions to embark on one more venture.

In the end he gave way, and applied once more to his good friend Benjamin Fletcher, Governor of New York, whose conception of right and wrong were somewhat elastic, for a privateering commission which was readily granted in return for a bribe of £300.

Tew now refitted the *Amity,* and in company with three other sloops reached Lipanan Island in the Red Sea, where his fleet was increased by one of "Long Ben" Avery's ships.

Here they fell in with a convoy of five Arab vessels. Tew attacked one of them but his luck had deserted him and in the battle that followed he was killed.

13
A Quartet of Sea Hawks

"Who do you choose as your captain?" asked the boatswain of the English merchantman.

"Brasiliano! Brasiliano!" the crew shouted eagerly.

Roch Brasiliano stepped forward. "I thank ye, lads. You'll not regret electing me. We'll sail together under the Jolly Roger and see if we can't prize plenty of gold out of the Spaniards—and anybody else who comes our way."

The crew of the ship on which Brasiliano had served as a common seaman had just mutinied, as so many crews did in those days, and had seized the ship. Their next step was then to choose a captain, and Brasiliano had already made himself popular and shown qualities of leadership.

Within days of being elected he had taken a galleon coming from New Spain, plundering her of a vast amount of gold and silver ingots. Then the ship sailed for Jamaica where Brasiliano and his crew squandered their loot in the taverns of Port Royal, that hotbed of vice and debauchery.

He decided to put to sea again, bought himself a ship with what was left of his share of the prize, and advertised for a crew.

"You know me," he said to those who applied. "Come with me and there'll be riches for all."

Rogues and cutthroats flocked to him, attracted by the reputation which he already had as a successful marauder.

Brasiliano planned to ransack the city of Campeche, in Mexico, but the news of his intention leaked out and he and his men were defeated after a short battle.

They were sent as prisoners to Spain. "You'll never keep me!" Brasiliano boasted to his captors—and they didn't.

Soon he had escaped and made his way back to Jamaica where he became leader of a combined pirate fleet of sloops and schooners, harassing the Spanish settlements, pillaging their towns and taking huge sums as ransom from the citizens.

What became of him afterwards we do not know for certain except the rumor that he was hanged at Gallows Reach at Port Royal.

"Discharged through insufficient evidence," was the judge's decision when Welshman Howel Davis was tried at Barbados for piracy.

Davis sneered behind his hand at the law which he regarded as a fool, and immediately headed for the island of New Providence where he hoped to join a marauding expedition.

He was disappointed to discover that most of the pirates whom he expected to meet had accepted the Act of Pardon recently brought from England by Captain Woodes Rogers.

Since Davis was urgently in need of money he joined a trading sloop bound for Martinique. Merely being a seaman, however, was not much in his line. He soon incited the crew to mutiny and seized the ship.

Once in command he altered course and made for the

Azores where he hoped to meet with trading ships carrying merchandise from Europe to the Dutch and Portuguese settlements on the West African coast.

On the way there a sail was spied to the windward and the pirates gave chase. When they came up with the vessel it was recognized as a Frenchman and Davis let fly the Skull and Crossbones.

When the dreaded flag was sighted the Frenchman set all canvas to escape but Davis's more agile sloop soon caught up, and after broadsides were exchanged, which did little harm to either vessel, the French ship struck her colors.

Davis took all arms and ammunition out of her and restored the ship to the captain as she was too cumbersome for his own purposes.

He next cruised down the Guinea coast until he came to Gambia where he carried out a colossal bluff.

Leaving only a few men on deck he ordered the rest of the crew below. He then cast anchor close to the fort and raised the Union Jack. Rowing ashore with a landing party he called on the Governor who greeted him in a friendly manner and listened sympathetically to Davis's tale that his ship was a Liverpool merchantman and that he had narrowly escaped from pirates.

" 'Twas a near thing, sir," he said. "Those pirates are fiends!"

"You must dine with me tonight," the Governor suggested. "Bring two of your officers."

Back on the ship Davis rubbed his hands with glee. "This fool will regret that he ever saw us. Muster every man on deck and I will explain my plan."

Davis told them all how he proposed to plunder the settlement; and later that evening he went ashore accompanied by the ship's surgeon and the first mate, taking with them a hamper of liquor as a present.

"It is mighty kind of you, sir, to break bread with us simple sailors," Davis said in his oily manner as they sat with the Governor at his table.

"I am sorry that I have not much fare to offer," the Governor replied.

The meal progressed, and then, at a signal from Davis, he and the surgeon leapt to their feet and sprang at the astonished Governor.

Davis kicked the chair from under him and quickly they had their host bound and gagged. Then Davis seized a lantern and waved it to and fro three times in the window which faced onto the harbor.

The boatswain on the sloop, seeing this, immediately set off shorewards in the longboat, taking a detachment of men and charging the guardroom. Taking the sentries by surprise and disarming them they soon had the place under control.

Davis now joined his men and the fort was plundered, the cannon sealed up and all other weapons transferred to the sloop.

In the morning they were about to sail when a ship appeared round the headland.

"Man the cannons!" Davis ordered. "Up with the Jolly Roger!"

But almost at the same time the approaching ship raised its own flag—and it, too, was the Skull and Crossbones.

Davis and his crew breathed a sigh of relief, and as the other vessel came within hailing distance they discovered that it was a French pirate commanded by Captain La Bourse.

The Frenchman and Davis drank and talked on board the sloop, and agreed that they should join forces and sail down the coast in search of prizes.

However, the first ship they met proved to be yet another pirate lying at anchor in the harbor of Sierra Leone. Her captain threw in his lot with them, and after a successful combined attack on a fort which yielded much booty the trio continued towards Accra; but shortly afterwards they quarrelled and parted company.

On the way to Suamabo Davis fought with three vessels of different nationalities all of which surrendered to him. He took from them what was of use to him and strengthened his crew with volunteers who joined him. He then let the ships go, except a Dutchman which he took for his own use, giving her the name *Rover*. The very next day he captured a rich prize worth fifteen thousand pounds.

Arriving at Accra he hoisted the English colors and sent the boatswain with a message to the Governor telling him that he was an English privateer charged with hunting pirates.

The Governor gave him a warm welcome and presented him with a variety of foodstuffs.

Davis now called his officers together in his cabin and outlined a plan which he hoped would bring them greater riches.

"We've got twelve Negro slaves on board; I'm going to send them to the Governor as a present in return for his hospitality. At the same time I shall invite him and all the members of his council to come on board for an entertainment. Once here we'll hold them to ransom. Forty thousand pounds I reckon they should be worth."

But this plan misfired, and proved to be fatal for

Davis. One of the slaves overheard the plot and in the night the Negro slipped overboard and swam ashore where he warned the Governor.

The next day, when Davis went ashore with his invitation the Governor greeted him cordially.

"Come into the fort and take wine with me," he said.

Davis, unsuspecting, accepted; but on entering the fort a shot from one of the guards killed him instantly.

The Robin Hood of the Ocean was the name often given to the Frenchman Ravenaux de Luson, and he seems to have deserved it.

No bloodcurdling stories sully his name, and of tales of chivalry towards his captives there are many.

This aristocratic sea-robber was of noble descent and had all the marks of a gentleman of high birth.

Dark ringlets fell to his shoulders, big black eyes sparkled in a well-formed face and upwards curled lips seemed to smile in mocking derision.

Not a "professional" in the true meaning of the word, he looked upon pirating as a diverting and profitable game during which he committed acts of reckless daring and valor.

He was an excellent writer and published a volume of his adventures on the high seas.

When he tired of the gay life of Paris he turned to piracy for a spell and is said to have amassed a great fortune by his robberies but had the reputation of treating his victims as guests rather than as captives.

When Captain Woodes Rogers arrived on the island of New Providence in 1718, carrying a Royal Pardon for all pirates who surrendered by a certain date, many hundreds of them took advantage of the chance to retire on their profits. Not so John Rackham, known as Calico Jack.

This hardened desperado sneeringly defied the act of clemency and sailed away towards the coast of Hispaniola.

"Fools may surrender themselves but not I!" he declared. "I'd wander the seas alone if necessary."

Breathing defiance he sought for prey, and soon seized a large London merchantman, the *Kingston,* laden with rich booty. Shifting some of his crew on board Calico Jack decided to keep her for his own. The loot was divided by throwing dice, and much of it was buried on the shores of an uninhabited island.

Then Calico Jack seems to have had a mysterious change of mind. He and his crew heard that the time limit for the Royal Pardon had been extended, and they decided to return to New Providence and take advantage of it. Perhaps the fact that they now had a lot of loot caused them to do this.

Whatever the reason, Calico Jack, having received his Certificate of Mercy, sold the *Kingston* and settled down to private life.

It was now that Anne Bonney entered the scene. Probably he was already weary of the quiet life even within a short time, and Anne persuaded him to get together some of his former crew and seize a sloop which lay in the harbor.

They spent some time in Cuba, living riotously and making frequent marauding expeditions.

One afternoon, just as they were about to sail, a Spanish coastguard ship came towards them, accompanied by a small English sloop which had just been captured.

Calico Jack took refuge in one of the narrow channels where the much heavier Spanish ship could not follow. While hiding there he thought of a clever idea.

In dead of night he launched his long-boat, put his crew into it and rowed silently up to the English sloop.

Shouting bloodthirsty oaths the pirates swarmed onto the sloop, killed the Spanish guard and tossed their bodies overboard, then quickly they hoisted sail and gained the open sea.

But Calico Jack's freedom was not to last for long.

Shortly afterwards, cruising off the western coast of Jamaica, he was challenged by a sloop sent out by the Governor of the island. After a heated fight Calico Jack was taken prisoner. Accused and found guilty of piracy he was hanged at Cape Corso Castle on the Guinea Coast.

14
Gallant John Lafitte

Mystery surrounds both the early life and eventual sudden disappearance of Jean Lafitte, most picturesque of corsairs, courteous to male prisoners, gallant to women.

Victor of more than a hundred pirate raids and heroic fighter for American freedom, Lafitte was born in St. Malo, in Brittany. He served as a youth on a French East Indiaman and graduated from privateer to pirate.

We hear of him first in the early part of the nineteenth century when piracy was already in decline, so that he was virtually the last of the notorious pirate chiefs. The growth of law and order and better working conditions aboard ship was putting an end to such as he.

The mouth of the Mississippi River off the Louisiana coast was his favorite hunting ground, with headquarters on the island of Grand Terre from where he played havoc with Spanish and American shipping.

Lafitte had influential friends in New Orleans who protected him from persecution. He also had an understanding with leading merchants in the city who bought the plundered treasures without question, and within a short time he had amassed a fortune.

He was a man of reckless daring, a supreme leader, resourceful when the odds were against him. By all accounts he was a dashing figure, his clothes immaculate and of the latest cut. He had the manners of a gentleman and knew well the effect that he created on other people.

During the war between Britain and the young United States, in 1814, the British had concentrated their forces around the mouth of the Mississippi in preparation for an attack on New Orleans.

They sent agents to Lafitte and said to him, "Captain, if you will help us capture New Orleans we will reward you well."

The Frenchman replied smoothly, "How well?"

"We offer you £30,000 and a captaincy in His Majesty's Navy."

"I will think about this. You must give me time."

Lafitte continued to make a play at negotiating with the British while secretly informing the Governor of New Orleans and offering his aid if the United States would grant him and his men a free pardon for their acts of piracy.

General Andrew Jackson, in command of the U.S. forces, realized that in view of the enemy's superiority in strength he could do with some help; accordingly he agreed to Lafitte's terms.

In the battle which followed the pirates fought side by side with the Americans and attacked the British so fiercely that they were forced to retreat.

The American Government kept its promise and granted pardons to Lafitte and his crew. But retirement in the luxury of New Orleans soon began to seem tame. The tang of the sea and the whiff of gunpowder haunted his dreams, and soon Lafitte was away raiding again.

The U.S. Government was forced to send a warship

Captain Bartholomew Roberts. (See Chapter 12)

Pirates carousing after successful plunder.

Captured pirate captain taken to commander of a British sloop.

William Dampier. (See Chapter 16)

George Clifford, Earl of Cumberland. A gentleman pirate. (*See Chapter 16*)

The death of Captain Kidd, by hanging in chains, May 23, 1701.
(*See Chapter 3*)

Pirate being hanged at Execution Dock.

François L'Olonois. (See Chapter 12)

Spanish ship sinking Buccaneer sloop.

Captain John Avery. (See Chapter 11)

to catch him, but Lafitte eluded his pursuers and thereafter vanished from the pages of history.

Was he lost in a storm? Or did he settle on some island in the sun there to live out his life in disguise? We shall never know.

15
Frederick Misson: The Good Pirate

Stealthily, through the dark jungle trails, long columns of painted savages advanced towards the cluster of dwellings.

Carrying spears, bows and arrows and deadly blowpipes loaded with darts dipped in fatal poison, they circled the clearing, awaiting the signal to attack.

Suddenly, the moon emerged from behind a cloud and shone its cold light for the last time upon the village of Liberatia, a socialist utopia founded before the word socialist was even known.

There it slumbered, peaceful in the eleventh and final year of its existence. Well-kept gardens surrounded the trim bungalows, the single street was stone-flagged; the moonlight glinted on the windows of the grocery store, the hardware shop, the seed merchant's.

A savage chief stood up, gave a mighty shout, and raced towards the village. From the trees his followers poured in their merciless hundreds, lusting for the kill. The dream of a perfect human society built by Frederick Misson died that night on Madagascar in the year 1720.

Misson was one of the strangest of all the figures in piratical history. Born in the region of France known as Provence he was intended for a military career. His family were wealthy and sent him to a military academy at

Angiers; but after a short spell there he decided that he preferred to go to sea.

Accordingly he joined a French man-of-war called the *Victoire* under the command of his uncle. It was during a trading cruise in the Mediterranean that Misson visited Rome, and there met a man as unusual as himself—an unfrocked priest named Caraccioli who held unconventional ideas about the priesthood and shared the theories about a new society which Misson was then developing; theories which today we would call socialistic.

Misson suggested that his new friend should join the *Victoire,* and his uncle was persuaded to agree. It was the beginning of a lifelong friendship filled with adventures shared by both.

While the *Victoire* was refitting before sailing for the West Indies Misson obtained leave to cruise on his own account in a borrowed sloop in the English Channel where he held up a merchant ship, taking from her many valuables but treating the captain with the utmost civility.

Shortly afterwards he took two Turkish pirates after a fierce fight. When he discovered on boarding them that they contained nothing valuable he let them go. On both occasions Caraccioli distinguished himself as a brave and valiant fighter despite his background as a priest.

Both men rejoined the *Victoire* at Brest where Misson sold the captured prizes and freed his prisoners. The *Victoire* then sailed for the West Indies.

Off Martinique they encountered an English man-of-war, the *Winchelsea,* which challenged and steadily gained upon her. On coming within hailing distance the *Winchelsea* hoisted the English colors to which the *Victoire* replied by raising the tricolor.

The enemy lay to and let go a broadside which killed

the captain and three officers of the *Victoire*. The situation looked grim. Caraccioli said a prayer. Was this to be the end of their venture?

Suddenly, without warning or apparent reason, the *Winchelsea* exploded in a blinding flash of scarlet flame and great clouds of smoke.

The *Victoire* was saved.

Misson and Caraccioli were now the only officers left and the crew elected the one captain and the other first lieutenant.

Misson called the men on deck and suggested that they turn pirate. He asked all to bind themselves together by a solemn oath to abide by a code of rules to be drawn up among them, to conduct all affairs in a humane and gentlemanly fashion and to abstain from all cruelties towards captured prisoners.

Without exception everyone cheered and all agreed to throw in their lot with his.

The *Victoire* sailed on and some days later sighted and captured a sloop of unknown nationality which they plundered and then freed.

When they were off St. Christopher a square-rigged craft came into sight and began to chase them. It proved to be a Jamaican privateer.

The evening was late and the *Victoire* lost sight of the enemy in the gathering darkness, but, expecting an attack at midnight, preparations were made.

As expected, at the change of the midnight watch the privateer stole alongside in an attempt to take the *Victoire* by surprise.

All seemed quiet on deck where Misson's crew were hidden awaiting the onslaught. As the attackers crept onto the deck they were quickly pounced upon and disarmed. Not one was killed.

Misson entertained the captain in his cabin and told him that he had given orders to his crew forbidding them to plunder the vessels and that his only request was for ammunition and small arms to be handed over. This was done and both parted on the best of terms.

The *Victoire* continued to Cartagena and Porto Bello. On the way she engaged two Dutch traders. Running close Misson fired all his guns on the larger vessel, bringing down her topmast and opening a gap in the side which sent her to the bottom.

The pirates then boarded the other ship, swarming into the rigging, flourishing cutlasses and pistols and gaining the deck.

The Dutch sailors fought valiantly but, realizing that further resistance was useless, eventually had to surrender.

The pirates found large quantities of bales of silk, rare spices from the East, precious garments of brocade and velvets, provisions and kegs of rum.

Misson decided to sell these goods at Cartagena, and to avoid suspicion as to the origin of the loot he evolved a clever plan.

The names of the captain of the Dutch vessel being Fourbim and that of the blown-up English frigate *D'Aubigny*, Misson and Caraccioli took these names and forged themselves papers.

Going ashore they presented themselves to the Governor, producing also a forged Letter of Marque from the French Admiralty authorizing them to attack English shipping.

The Governor received the two in friendly manner and sent local merchants to board the *Victoire* and buy the loot at profitable prices. In return Misson sent the Governor a present of brocade.

A decision now had to be made about the future. Misson called the crew together and made a speech.

They were not pirates, he told them, but brave upstanding men determined to fight against oppression and poverty; their cause was that of liberty. Like all other men they had equal rights before a divine being.

These sentiments were loudly applauded by the crew, and it was decided to sail to African waters and cruise down the west coast in search of pirates.

The journey was uneventful until one morning, as the wind freshened, a two-masted brigantine was sighted in the clearing mist.

The alarm was given and the *Victoire* took up the chase. She steadily gained upon the frigate which suddenly hove to and opened fire, causing no great damage.

Misson replied with a thunderous broadside which riddled the frigate's timbers and shattered her rudder. Clustered round their captain the crew of the frigate fought gallantly until a musket shot killed him. Only then did they surrender.

The prisoners were treated with the usual consideration and their captain buried on shore with a stone over his grave bearing the inscription "Here lies a brave Englishman."

Misson took £60,000 from the frigate and invited those of the crew who wished to do so to join him. Thirty did so, first swearing that they would not be dissolute or immoral in their behavior.

With his fleet of four vessels Misson rounded the Cape and headed for the island of Madagascar in the Indian Ocean, intent on realizing a dream which he had had for some time—the dream of establishing a colony in which all would be equal and free and Christian principles would be observed.

Landing on Madagascar he called his men together and addressed them once again.

"Here we shall live and call our town Liberatia. All shall be bound together by mutual trust and every man shall enjoy perfect freedom."

"What about property?" someone asked.

"No man shall own any property, and all money shall be kept in a common fund in the care of an elected council. Here we shall dwell in peace and friendship the like of which the world outside cannot know."

And so Liberatia was built. Houses were constructed and a fort erected on either side of the harbor entrance, protected by cannon from the captured ships.

In spite of the different nationalities of the settlers there was no language problem. Misson invented a kind of Esperanto made up of French, Dutch, English and Portuguese words.

As mentioned in an earlier chapter Misson was joined by the American pirate Tew and the lives of the two men became closely linked.

Then came that terrible night when the natives, previously friendly, descended on the little township. Tew was away at the time on a raiding expedition and so was not involved.

Why the natives rose we shall never know, but they burned Liberatia to the ground after it had thrived for ten years. Most of the inhabitants were killed.

Misson and a few comrades managed to flee in one of their sloops, but it was caught in a hurricane and foundered. All were drowned.

So ended the pirate utopia.

16
Pirates in All but Name

Roaming the oceans of the New World that Spain haughtily claimed for her own, Britain's sea dogs battered and looted the great treasure-laden galleons of the Dons in the sixteenth century.

It was the Elizabethan age: the age of Drake and Hawkins and Raleigh; men who were pirates in all but name and who made the British flag feared by its enemies.

The plundering of merchant vessels bent on legitimate trade but sailing under unfriendly colors was looked upon as a profession and not as a crime.

Although the governments of England and France publicly disapproved of the practice, in secret they condoned and even encouraged it.

They provided adventurers with cunningly worded Letter Patents authorizing them to stop and seize ships belonging to nations with which they were at war at the time.

Even in periods when a formal peace existed between England and Spain there were always daring spirits prepared to attack vessels sailing under her flag.

Such actions were little less than piracy, but were prompted by a burning sense of patriotism and an intense hatred of a Spain which arrogantly denied the right of English merchants to trade with the New World.

Treaty or no treaty this meant a constant state of thinly disguised warfare. English and French marauders often buried their own prejudices and united against Spain.

It is not surprising that Spain looked upon the two countries as nests of pirates that had to be destroyed, with England as the archvillain. To strike a deadly blow the Great Armada was sent against England's shores—and was shattered by the hated nation of pirates.

Leading figures among the Gentlemen Adventurers were Hawkins, Drake, the Duke of Cumberland, Raleigh, Rupert of the Rhine and, later, Dampier.

When their piratical ventures met with success a grateful government treated them as national heroes; if they failed the Crown denied all knowledge of their deeds.

Courage and enterprise were the outstanding qualities of men such as Drake and Hawkins. Both West Countrymen, with the spirit of the sea in their veins, they were partly pioneers, partly freebooters, not troubled by any questions about the rights and wrongs of international conduct. Life in those Elizabethan days was tough, and the actions of these men have to be judged against the background of their times.

John Hawkins started the notorious trade in African slaves called "Black Ivory," which yielded immense profits and which he carried out with the Queen's consent. So profitable were his trading exploits that Elizabeth chose him and Drake to lead a marauding party against the Spanish settlements in the New World. Their exploits in attacking and ransacking Spanish towns and harassing Spanish vessels were highly successful and they were always graciously welcomed by Elizabeth when they returned home laden with rich cargoes of gold and silver and plundered booty. Although she could not openly approve of such ventures, she secretly sponsored and invested money in them.

After an attack on the Spanish fleet off Vera Cruz ended in disaster, from which but one of the English ships escaped, Hawkins spent some time in semi-retirement, but Elizabeth's confidence in her admiral was not shaken.

From what we know of Francis Drake, blunt honesty and a restless energy were the hallmarks of his character. He was described as gallant and chivalrous, with courtly manners. He enjoyed the confidence of Elizabeth, who sent him out in 1570 in command of a fleet to ravage the Spanish cities and seize their ships, even though England was officially at peace with Spain at the time.

Drake justified the Queen's expectations. In a brilliant land and sea campaign he sacked the city of Cartagena, which was the storehouse of Spain's wealth in America, in spite of its apparently impregnable situation, surrounded by swampy jungle and treeless sandy shores.

His greatest triumph was the ambushing of convoys of packmule trains which crossed the Isthmus of Panama laden with gold and silver from Inca mines in Peru on their way to the mouth of the Chagres River, from where the treat galleons took it to Spain. The value of the loot which Drake brought to England is believed to have reached the enormous sum of £8 million.

In the years 1577 to 1580 Drake circumnavigated the globe in the *Golden Hind,* his flagship of a puny hundred tons—a feat that had never before been done.

The journey was supposed to have been undertaken for the discovery of new lands, but its real purpose was to attack Spanish property in the Americas.

Drake captured a galleon from which he took a booty of solid gold weighing 400 pounds and seized another treasure ship carrying 20 tons of precious metals, pearls and diamonds estimated to be worth 1½ million Sterling.

Elizabeth was delighted with the brilliant achievements of her bold adventurer, but she found it tactful to abstain from honoring him publicly in view of Spain's demands that he be punished for piratical exploits committed during a time when friendly relations existed between her and England.

The Queen pretended to be greatly shocked and displeased with her admiral's misdeeds and ordered the *Golden Hind* to be put in drydock at Plymouth. At her counsellors' advice she ordered Drake's temporary retirement from public life, hoping to pacify Spain's anger thereby.

The magnificence of Drake's presents, however, caused Elizabeth to call him to court after the lapse of a few short months, and when she attended a banquet which Drake gave on board the *Golden Hind* she bestowed a knighthood on him.

Having achieved the height of his fame with the defeat of the Armada, disaster overtook him. In the year 1596 Drake set out once more on a raiding venture against the Spanish settlements in the Caribbean and along the South American coast but they found the places well garrisoned and amply fortified. Their attacks were ineffective and in an onslaught on one of the towns Hawkins was mortally wounded while Drake was killed in the following year.

On a dark night a flotilla of ships drifted silently to

anchorage outside the harbor mouth off Porto Rico. Ashore flickered the lights of the town of San Juan.

In the darkness men clambered down the sides of the ships into small boats and rowed quietly ashore in two detachments which landed and approached to within a mile of the sleeping town. Then, at dawn, the order came to attack. Swarming into the streets they took the inhabitants by surprise. People fled in terror or surrendered on the spot, not realizing that the attacking force was in fact only small.

Porto Rico itself was taken after but a brief fight, thus making another daring success for George, Earl of Cumberland, one of the outstanding figures of the Elizabethan age and a brilliant strategist.

A Cambridge scholar and expert sailor, Knight of the Order of the Garter, keen sportsman and reckless gambler, smooth courtier and strict disciplinarian, yet he was jovial to those under him and humane to his prisoners.

Wealthy as he was he did not need to make money by piracy. His motive was patriotism and a universal hatred of Spain which dominated the English upper classes.

After establishing himself in Porto Rico he intended to use it as a permanent base from which to wreck Spanish trade in the New World. His plans however were defeated by an outbreak of yellow fever which killed more than half of his men and forced him to return to England.

Another Gentleman Adventurer of Queen Elizabeth's time was Sir Walter Raleigh, national hero of the people. Like other of the country's most intrepid seamen of that period—Hawkins, Drake, Gilbert, Morgan—he came from the West Country, with the sea in his veins.

Entirely fearless and brave in combat, he had amazing energy and an indomitable spirit which spurred on those under him. He was the subject of stories of deeds of valor and daring already during his lifetime and his achievements as a colonizer have passed into history.

It has been said of Raleigh that he was little more than a pirate but all the great sea-rovers of the era, with few exceptions, if not pirates in the true sense were men whose actions showed a marked disregard for the property of their fellow men.

There is little doubt that Raleigh committed acts of brigandage. However, judging by the terms of the age in which he lived, it is small wonder that a certain laxity of principles was looked upon with tolerance.

Raleigh was a strange mixture of filibuster and explorer, courtier and fighting man, poet and historian.

Educated at Oxford and the Temple, he had all the qualities of a cultured man of letters. He was tall, handsome and debonair, and with his courtly manners ingratiated himself into the good graces of Queen Elizabeth.

Everyone knows the pretty story of his gallantry when he spread his coat for the Queen to step over. Whether the tale is true or not it adds a picturesque touch to a picturesque personality.

Unfortunately he fell from royal favor for a time when an affair which he was said to have had with one of Elizabeth's maids of honor led to his imprisonment in the Tower of London.

On his release Raleigh went to sea in the service of his country, filled with the burning desire to aid the cause against the hated Spaniards with whom England was in a state of undeclared war.

He came to blows with them on sea and land and caused immense damage to their ocean-born trade, seizing and plundering rich cargoes plying back and forth across the Caribbean, sacking and burning towns and villages, ambushing caravans which carried gold and silver from the mines in Peru across the Isthmus for shipment to Spain.

In 1578, together with his half-brother Humphrey Gilbert, the founder of the first British colony in North America, Raleigh joined a piratical expedition which swept the Main in search of prey. He made invasions on land, attacked and assaulted settlements and ransacked cities, storming and capturing their fortified batteries; although the Spanish troops nearly always outnumbered his fighting men he never hesitated to engage them in bitter combat.

His successes at sea were no less spectacular. Laying in wait along the route of huge Europe-bound galleons loaded to the gunwales with treasure he swept down on them; he boarded and disabled lumbering trading vessels and took prizes all the way from the Bahamas to the Guinea Gulf.

Returned to England he was accused and condemned for alleged conspiracy against King James and sent to the Tower once again. After thirteen years of confinement the King ordered his release, prompted by Raleigh's fantastic stories of a mythical El Dorado abounding in untold riches which he promised to find.

The King appointed him leader of an ill-equipped expedition which came to grief at the mouth of the Orinoco River. Empty-handed and poor in health, Raleigh went home, where he was arrested on an old charge of piracy. His execution a year later is common history.

Prince Rupert, Count Paladine of the Rhine, saw service as a general under Charles I and as an admiral under

Charles II. He was a dashing cavalier, handsome and with a soldierly figure. Already in his early life the prince had had a constant round of romantic adventures. His character was a strange mixture of romance, enthusiasm and shrewd stoicism. He succeeded in controlling his fiery temper by a careful restraint of acting on the spur of the moment. He was restless and full of nervous energy, impetuous and headstrong. His mind was swift and alert and his courage undaunted.

When his military career under Charles I ended his spirit called for fresh adventures, and in 1648, accompanied by his brother Maurice, he cruised the Caribbean in command of a privateering fleet of seven vessels but soon found the irksome restrictions which a letter of marque imposed upon the holder too slow and unexciting an affair.

Realizing that legal crusading could not satisfy his boundless energy he decided to go freebooting on his own. It is possible that his decision to join the pirates was prompted more by a desire for adventure than for the sake of wealth.

Prince Rupert was skilled in naval warfare. He was the first to suggest the strategy for a fleet to advance in battle and engage the enemy instead of awaiting the attack.

The career of this royal filibuster, though merry and exciting, lasted a bare five years in which he met with every kind of adventure. He never committed acts of cruelty or forgot his good manners as a gentleman.

The end was quick and final. On one of his marauding expeditions Rupert's vessels were caught in a storm off the Virgin Islands which drove them onto the rocks. There were few survivors and among those drowned was his brother Maurice.

Weary and broken in spirit the Prince returned to the coast of France in the only vessel that had escaped from sinking. From there he reached England where he lived for some years in obscurity. He died unnoticed, his meteoric career forgotten.

A superb navigator who followed in the footsteps of Drake at a later period in history was William Dampier. Up to then it had been the Spaniards who had made the great voyages of discovery in unknown parts of the globe.

Born the son of a Somerset farmer, Dampier had all kinds of adventures in his time. He was in turn, freebooter and pirate, famous explorer and naturalist, distinguished Naval officer and eminent author.

At the age of seventeen he sailed as apprentice on a merchantman to the West Indies where he deserted and joined a party of pirates led by Bartholomew Sharp with whom he crossed the Isthmus of Darien, taking part in the sacking and burning of towns and the rounding up of prisoners as hostages for the payment of ransom.

Disgusted by the cruelties meted out to them by his fellow pirates, he left their company and tried his hand at farming in Jamaica but found this too unexciting a profession and signed on with the crew of a privateering vessel bent on an expedition to Australia.

Having an inquiring mind for geographical and natural features, he made copious notes which he published on his return to England. They caught the attention of the Admiralty who fitted out a frigate and commissioned him to explore along the northwest coasts of Australia and New Guinea.

In 1683 Dampier accompanied Captain John Cook as sailing master of the privateer *Revenge* round Cape Horn, no mean feat with the type of craft then in use.

Buccaneering exploits to Sierra Leone and the coast of Brazil followed and in 1699 he was a member of an expedition sent by the Admiralty under the command of Woodes Rogers on a voyage round the world. Landing at the San Juan Fernandez Islands the marooned sailor Alexander Selkirk, Defoe's immortal Robinson Crusoe, was discovered and rescued.

Tolerant as a rule, he could be strict and austere in the handling of his crews and there is an incident on record where a charge of cruelty towards his men was lodged which led to his being brought before a Naval tribunal; but he met this with the explanation that he had been faced with mutiny and had to repress it with an iron hand.

Dampier was one of the great figures in the history of overseas discoveries and a pioneer of scientific exploration. He was the first naturalist who gave a description of a typhoon. In addition to several books on natural history he published his *Voyage Round the World* in 1697 and a *A Discovery of Winds* two years later.

On his last journey his vessel foundered and was wrecked on Ascension Island but he was rescued and taken to England by an East Indiaman. He died in London.

17
Postscript

The age of piracy is gone. Born of evil social conditions at sea and on land it is now neither necessary nor practical.

The modern sailor, with decent pay, trade unions and humane conditions, does not have the incentive to turn pirate; and with radio, radar and aircraft at the disposal of governments it would be impossible to escape afterwards anyway.

The story of piracy makes romantic reading, but it was not very romantic at the time.

Life is better as it is today.

Types of Old Seagoing Craft

BRIGANTINE: two-masted trading vessel.
FRIGATE: naval craft mounted with cannon and guns.
GALLEON: large, heavy vessel used by the Spaniards.
KETCH: small two-masted vessel of about 100 tons burden.
LONG-BOAT: a large boat carried by a ship.
PINNACE: light man-of-war's rowing boat.
SCHOONER: a two- or three-masted vessel.
SHALLOP: light open boat used in shallow water.
SLOOP: one-, two-, or three-masted vessel furnished with guns or light falconets firing small shot and scrap iron.

Bibliography

John Esquemeling. *The Buccaneers of America.* (1678)
C. H. Haring. *The Buccaneers in the West Indies.*
Captain Charles Johnson. *General History of the Robberies and Murders of the Most Notorious Pirates.* (1724)
C. Leslie. *A History of Jamaica.*
C. H. Rarraker. *The Hispaniola Treasure.*
George Roberts. *The Four Voyages of Captain George Roberts.* (1726)
Woodes Rogers. *A Cruising Voyage Round the World.* (1712)

Index

Accra, 107
Adventure, 47
Adventure Galley, 26, 28, 30
American Colonies, 27
American Liberator, 70
"Amity," The, 101, 102
Anamaboa, 91
Angiers, 115
Arabian Coast, 100
Arab Vessels, 102
Archbishop of York, 63
Armada, 13, 122, 124
Ascension Island, 130
Attila the Hun, 58
Australia, 129
Avery, Captain John, 86–90, 99, 100, 102
Azores, 105

Bahamas, 41, 48, 52, 74, 79, 127
Barbados, 46, 93, 104
Bartholomew Island, 94
Bath, 51
Bay of Honduras, 46
Belmont, Lord, 27, 31–34
Bibliography, 133
Blackbeard, 44, 79
Black Bunting, 40, 92, 100
Blackburne, Lancelot, 63
Black Flag, 45, 47, 72, 79, 80
Black Ivory, 122
Bloodthirsty Wenches, 72
Bolivar, Simon, 70
Bonito, Benito, 70
Bonney, Anne, 72–74, 80, 82, 109

Borneo, 43
Boston, 31, 89
Boucan, 22
Brasiliano, Roch, 103
Breda, 78
Brethren of the Coast, 80
———— of the Main, 24, 25, 64
———— of the Tortuga, 60
Brest, 115
Brinkinghorn, Captain, 69
Britain's War with France, 27
British Flag, 121
Brittany, 111
Bulwarks, 92
Buried Treasure, 27, 69, 70, 71
Buccaneers, 22, 23, 25, 38

Calico Jack, 80, 109, 110
Callao, 70
Cambridge Scholar, 125
Campbell, Sir Malcolm, 71
Campeche, 104
Cape Corso Castle, 110
Cape Lopez, 95
Cape of Good Hope, 101
Caraccioli, 115, 116
Caribbean, 8, 9, 13, 25, 38, 41, 63, 65, 93, 124, 127
Carolinas, 45, 49, 73
Cartagena, 25, 117, 123
Celebes, 43
Certificate of Mercy, 109
Cesspool of Christendom, 59
Chagres River, 15, 123
Charles I, 64, 127, 218

Charles II, 128
Charleston, 45, 48
Chile, 13
China Coast, 43
China Sea, 67
Chinese Woman Pirates, 84
Ching, Mrs., 84
Cobham, Maria, 73, 82, 83, 84
Cocos Island, 69, 70, 71
Cocos Treasure, 69, 70, 71
Coniers, Crown Counsel, 33
Cook, Captain John, 129
Corsairs, 62
Costa Rica, 69
County Cork, Ireland, 73
"Cow Killers," 23
Crusoe, Robinson, 64
Cuba, 75
Culliford, Captain Robert, 30, 34
Cumberland, George, Earl of, 122, 125

Dampier, William, 64, 122, 129, 130
Darien, 99
D'Aubigny, Captain, 117
Davis, Captain Edward, 70
Davis, Captain Havel, 91, 104
Deadlier than the Male, 72
Defoe, Daniel, 64
Deserters from the Services, 37
Discovery of Winds, A, 130
Dover's Powder, 65
Drake, Sir Francis, 24, 122, 124, 125, 129
Duke, The, 86–88
Dutch East India Co., 101
Dutch West India Co., 79

East India Co., 29
Eden, Charles, 51–53, 58
El Dorado, 127
Elizabeth I, Queen, 123, 124

Elizabethan Age, 121, 125
Elizabethan Sea Robbers, 91
Emmet, James, 31, 32
English Channel, 115
Ensign, 55
Esperanto, 119
Esquemeling, John, 9, 15, 16, 18–21
Etonian, Old, 65
Execution Dock, 42

Filibusters, 65
Fletcher, Benjamin, 101
Fortune, The, 94, 95
Fourbin, Captain, 117
Freebooters, 22, 24, 63, 75
Free Pardon, 31, 42, 45
French Admiralty, 117
French Passes, 31, 34

Galleons, 13, 19, 24, 39, 62, 68, 93, 103, 104
Gallows, 34
Gallows Point, 82
Gallows Reach, 104
Gambia, 105
Gentlemen Adventurers, 35, 122
Gentlemen of the King's Bedchamber, 64
Gentlemen Pirates, 62
George I, King, 42
Gilbert, Sir Humphrey, 125, 127
Golden Hind, 123, 124
Government of New York, 191
Grand Terre, 111
Great Mogul, 87, 88, 99, 101
Guayaquil, 64, 79
Guinea, 41
Guinea Coast, 94, 105, 110, 127
Gunner Moore, 26

Hands, Israel, 47, 50, 58
Haiti, 22
Havana, 48

INDEX

Hawkins, John, 24, 121, 122, 123, 125
Heweson, Colonel, 33
Hidden Treasure, 67
Hideout, 59
Highwayman, 65
Hispaniola, 8, 22, 23, 31, 32, 68
Honduras, 64
Hon-Cho-Lo, Mrs., 84
Horn, Cape, 129
Horngold, Captain Benjamin, 45, 46
House of Commons Journals, 32

Inca Mines, 123
Indian Princess, 90
Indus River, 87
Ireland, 89
Isthmus of Panama, 63, 123

Jackson, Andrew, 112
Jamaica, 21, 41, 59, 61, 72, 129
James I, King, 127
James River, 53
Johnson, Captain Charles, 9, 10, 90
Jolly Roger, 46, 91, 95, 103, 106
Juan Fernandez, 64

Kidd, Captain William, 26–34, 67
King's Enemies, 63
King's Pardon, 32, 54, 90
Kingston, The, 109
Knight, Charles, 58
Knight, Tobias, 53

La Bourse, Captain, 106
Lafitte, Jean, 111, 112, 113
Le Sieur Ravanau de Lussou, 65
Letter of Marque, 9, 36, 117
Letter of Patents, 121
Liberatia, 101, 114, 119

Lima, 70
Lipanon Island, 102
Lisbon, 92
Livingstone, Colonel, 28
L'Olonois, François, 96–99
Lodge, Thomas, M.D. (Cambridge Scholar), 64
Lodge, Thomas (Oxford Scholar), 63, 65
"Long Ben," 86
Long Island, 31
Lopez, Cape, 95
Lord Mayor of London, 63
Los Todas Santos, 92
Louisiana Coast, 111
Lutrelle, Prudence, 51

Madagascar, 26, 29, 30, 34, 86, 87, 99, 100, 101, 114, 119
Maracaibo, 96–98
Martinique, 52, 58, 94, 104, 115
Mary Dean, 70
Massachusetts, 68
Maynard, Lt. Robert, 53–56, 58
Mecca, 88, 101
Mediterranean, 115
Mexico, 104
Mississippi River, 111, 112
Misson, Frederick, 101, 114, 116–120
Morgan, Sir Henry, 7, 13–21, 25, 68, 125
Mutiny, 30

Nassau, 80
Nelson, Horatio, 36
New England, 27
Newfoundland, 70, 93, 94
New Guinea, 129
New Orleans, 111, 112
Newport, 101
New Providence, 45, 74, 80, 89, 109

Oak Island, 67, 71
Ocracoke, 51, 53
Ogle, Captain Chaloner, 95
Old Bailey, 32
Order of the Garter, 125
Orinoco River, 127
Oxford, Earl of, 28
Oxford Scholar, 63, 126

Pacific, 16
Pamlico Sound, 53
Panama, 13–16, 25, 65, 68, 69
Pathhoi District, 84
Peru, 13, 65, 68, 123, 127
Pieces of Eight, 41, 88
Pirate Aristocrat, 66
Pirates, Piracy, 8, 9, 37, 38, 62, 63, 65, 72, 131
Pirate Stronghold, 59
Pirate Utopia, 120
Phips, Sir William, 68
Plum Point, 52
Plymouth, 124
Porter, Endymion, 64
Porto Bello, 117
Porto Rico, 125
Port Royal, 42, 59, 60, 61, 103, 104
Portuguese Fleet, 92
Portuguese Settlements, 105
"Powder Monkey," 77
Princess (Slavetrader), 91
Prince Rupert, 128
Privateer, 24, 26, 35, 36, 50, 63, 107
Proclamation of Pardon, 42
Protection Racket, 66
Protestant Caesar, 47, 48
Provence, 114

Quedah, The, 30
Queen Anne's Revenge, 46, 49

Rampura, 87, 88

Rackham, Captain John, 72, 74, 75, 76, 80, 82, 109
Raleigh, Sir Walter, 121, 122, 125, 126, 127
Ranger, 95, 96
Ravenaux de Luson, 108
Read, Mary, 72, 73, 75, 76, 77, 80, 82
Red Sea, 87, 101, 102
Resolution, The, 30
Rhode Island, 100, 101
Richard, 47
Roberts, Captain Bartholomew, 91
Robin Hood of the Ocean, 108
Robinson Crusoe, 79
Rogers, Captain Woodes, 64, 79, 80, 108
Romney, Earl of, 28
Royal Commission, 28
Royal Pardon, 104, 109
Rupert of the Rhine, 122
Ryswick, Peace of, 78

St. Christopher, 22, 116
St. Iago de la Vega, 72
St. Kitts, 23
St. Malo, 111
Saluks (Moslem Sea Robbers), 39, 42, 43
San Jose, Church of, 14, 19
San Lorenzo, 13, 14, 20
Santo Domingo, 22
San Vincent, 46
Scarborough, The, 46
Sea-robbers, 39, 42, 43
Sharp, Bartholomew, 129
Shrewsburg, Duke of, 28
Sierra Leone, 95, 107
Simmons, Henry, 65
Sinful City, 59
Skull and Crossbones, 55, 67, 75, 105, 106
Slave Girls, 60

INDEX

Slave Trader, 91
Somers, Lord, 28
Spain, 8, 23, 38, 42, 60, 61, 62, 70, 103, 121, 123
Spanish Main, 8, 22, 62
Spanish Senoritas, 60
Spanish Settlement, 124
Spanish Town, 72
"Sparrow Shooting," 60
Spotswood, Governor of Virginia, 53, 54
Suamabo, 107
Successful Pirate, The, 90
Surinam River, 92

Teach, Edward, 44, 46
Terror of the Seas, 44
Temple, 126
Tew, 99, 100, 119
Thompson, Captain, 70
"Three Horseshoes," 78
Tortuga, 8, 13, 22, 24, 98
"Torturer," The, 96
Tortures, 38, 39
Tower of London, 126, 127
Treasure, Hidden, 66, 68
Treaty of Friendship, 21
Trepassi, Harbor of, 93
Trial of Captain John Rackham, 72

Trinity College, Oxford, 36
Trujillo, 47
Turkish Pirates, 115
Turneffe, 47
Types of Old Seagoing Craft, 132
Typhoon, A Description of a, 130

Union Jack, 105

Venezuela, 96
Vera Cruz, 123
Victoire, 115–118
Virgin Mary, 69
Virginia, 53, 58
Virgin Islands, 128
Voyage 'Round the World, 130

West African Coast, 105
West African Waters, 94
West Country, 125
West Indian Archipelago, 8, 24, 44, 45, 94
Whig Government, 33
William III, King, 28
Winchelsea, 115, 116
Windward Islands, 46
Wing Song (British Steamer), 43
Women Pirates, 72

Yucatan, 98, 99